HISTORY OF THE WORLD

The Americas in the Colonial Era

RSVP

RAINTREE
STECK-VAUGHN
P U B L I S H E R S
The Steck-Vaughn Company

Austin, Texas

TABLE OF CONTENTS

This book has been reviewed for accuracy by
Bruce Taylor, PhD., University of Dayton

Il Nuovo Mondo ©1991 by Editoriale Jaca Book, Milan

Italian text by Monica Dambrosio and Roberto Barbieri
Illustrations by Remo Berselli
English translation by Mary Di Ianni

Cover Illustration by Remo Berselli

Raintree Steck-Vaughn Editorial
Helene Resky: Editor

Raintree Steck-Vaughn Art/Production
D. Childress: Art Director
Cynthia Ellis: Production Manager

Electronic Production
Management by Design

Printed and bound in the United States of America

3 4 5 6 7 8 9 0 WO 98 97 96 95 94

Library of Congress Cataloging-in-Publication Data
Dambrosio, Monica
    [Il Nuovo mondo. English]
    The Americas in the Colonial era / [Italian text by Monica Dambrosio and Roberto Barbieri;
illustrations by Remo Berselli; English translation by Mary Di Ianni].
        p. cm. — [History of the world]
        Includes index.
        Summary: Surveys the history of North and South America from the pre-Columbian
civilizations' encounter with European explorers through the American Revolution.
        ISBN 0-8114-3326-9
        1. America – History – To 1810 – Juvenile literature. [1. America – History – To 1810.]
    I. Barbieri, Roberto, ill. II. Berselli, Remo. III. Title. IV. Series.

E18.82.D3613   1993
973.2 – dc20   92-19154
                                                          CIP
                                                          AC

A seafarer from Southwest Alaska. The Aleuts, who lived in this area, had broken away from the Eskimos earlier in their history and had developed a culture that depended on the sea.

A Native North American. Despite the continent's huge size, the North American Indian cultures could be divided into three major groups: the Eastern Woodland Indians, the Hunters of the Plains, and the Fishers of the North.

An Indian mask from the Northwest Coast (1500 B.C.). The coastal tribes were particularly famous for their ability to carve and decorate wood.

A Hopewell dignitary in ceremonial dress. The Hopewell civilization, (400 B.C.– A.D. 400) developed in the region of what is now central Ohio.

Chimecoatl, a pre-Columbian deity.

A Mayan sculpture of a priestess in front of a temple. The Mayan civilization, which began to develop around 500 B.C., was famous for its pottery. This civilization was already in decline at the beginning of the Spanish conquest.

Beaufort Sea

GREENLAND

Baffin Island

Alaska Range

Great Bear Lake

Great Slave Lake

Hudson Bay

Labrador

Newfoundland

Lake Winnipeg

St. Lawrence River

Columbia River

Rocky Mountains

Lake Superior

Lake Huron

Lake Michigan

Central Lowlands

Ohio River

Atlantic Ocean

Pacific Ocean

Sierra Nevada

Missouri River

Platte R.

Appalachian Mountains

Colorado R.

Arkansas R.

Canadian R.

Red R.

Mississippi R.

Baja California

Colorado R.

Brazos R.

Río Grande R.

Eastern Sierra Madre

Western Sierra Madre

Florida

Gulf of Mexico

Bahamas

Cuba

Hispaniola

Yucatan Peninsula

Caribbean Sea

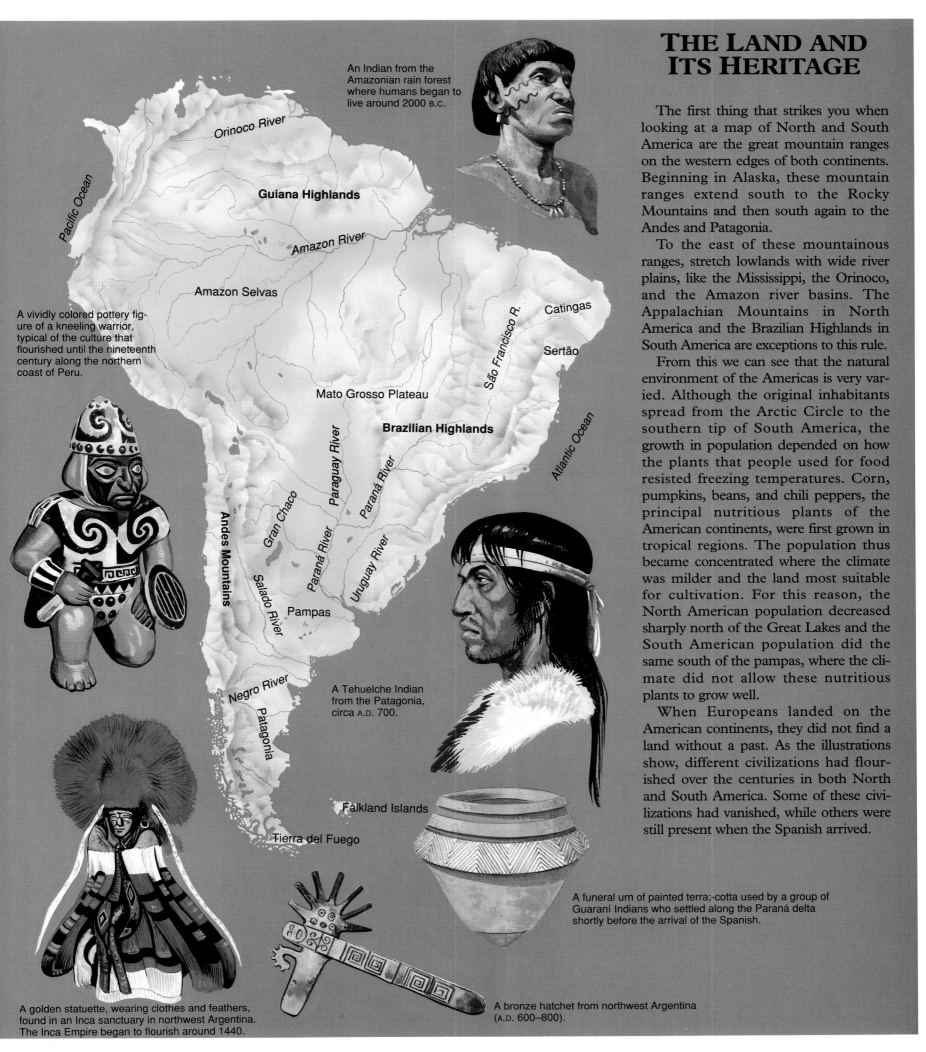

THE LAND AND ITS HERITAGE

An Indian from the Amazonian rain forest where humans began to live around 2000 B.C.

Orinoco River

Guiana Highlands

Pacific Ocean

Amazon River

Amazon Selvas

São Francisco R.

Catingas

Sertão

A vividly colored pottery figure of a kneeling warrior, typical of the culture that flourished until the nineteenth century along the northern coast of Peru.

Mato Grosso Plateau

Brazilian Highlands

Atlantic Ocean

Paraguay River

Paraná River

Andes Mountains

Gran Chaco

Paraná River

Uruguay River

Salado River

Pampas

Negro River

A Tehuelche Indian from the Patagonia, circa A.D. 700.

Patagonia

Falkland Islands

Tierra del Fuego

A golden statuette, wearing clothes and feathers, found in an Inca sanctuary in northwest Argentina. The Inca Empire began to flourish around 1440.

A bronze hatchet from northwest Argentina (A.D. 600–800).

A funeral urn of painted terra;-cotta used by a group of Guaraní Indians who settled along the Paraná delta shortly before the arrival of the Spanish.

The first thing that strikes you when looking at a map of North and South America are the great mountain ranges on the western edges of both continents. Beginning in Alaska, these mountain ranges extend south to the Rocky Mountains and then south again to the Andes and Patagonia.

To the east of these mountainous ranges, stretch lowlands with wide river plains, like the Mississippi, the Orinoco, and the Amazon river basins. The Appalachian Mountains in North America and the Brazilian Highlands in South America are exceptions to this rule.

From this we can see that the natural environment of the Americas is very varied. Although the original inhabitants spread from the Arctic Circle to the southern tip of South America, the growth in population depended on how the plants that people used for food resisted freezing temperatures. Corn, pumpkins, beans, and chili peppers, the principal nutritious plants of the American continents, were first grown in tropical regions. The population thus became concentrated where the climate was milder and the land most suitable for cultivation. For this reason, the North American population decreased sharply north of the Great Lakes and the South American population did the same south of the pampas, where the climate did not allow these nutritious plants to grow well.

When Europeans landed on the American continents, they did not find a land without a past. As the illustrations show, different civilizations had flourished over the centuries in both North and South America. Some of these civilizations had vanished, while others were still present when the Spanish arrived.

PRE-COLUMBIAN CIVILIZATIONS

The First Americans

Shortly before Christopher Columbus arrived in the Americas, millions of people already lived here. Columbus called these people "Indians" because he thought he had landed in the Indies, islands off the southeastern coast of Asia. In Mexico, Central America and in the Andes Mountains, some of the most magnificent civilizations the world has ever known had developed and flourished, totally unknown by the people in Europe and Asia at the time. Every type of culture was present in the Americas: primitive societies of hunters and gatherers; simple societies based on agriculture; and powerful empires. Today a great part of this ancient splendor is little more than a memory because the European settlers and conquerors destroyed the native populations. The Native Americans had little chance to save themselves as European technology was much more advanced than that of their own cultures.

At the time Columbus arrived, around four hundred languages were spoken in the Americas. With the exception of the Inuit language, no other link between any Native American language and the languages of Asia or Europe has been proven.

Scholars still disagree about how to estimate the total population and the exact number of languages spoken in the Americas, but most agree that people arrived on the American continent from Asia around thirty thousand years ago by crossing the Bering Strait. These first inhabitants of the American continent knew how to make objects and had acquired the skills to obtain food and shelter.

The Environment

The environment of the Americas is quite varied. There are huge mountains, broad plains, and river basins on both continents. It is impossible to generalize about places where the native population lived. Before the arrival of Columbus, people were distributed over the whole length of both continents, from Greenland, where the Inuit lived, to the tip of South America.

The growth of population and civilizations in the Americas was dependent on the ability of nutritious plants to resist frost. The principal plants – corn, pumpkins, beans, and chili – were in fact of tropical origin, and the population became concentrated where cultivation of these plants was easiest, that is, in the temperate latitudes. For example, in eastern North America, corn was grown as far north as the Great Lakes, beyond which the population suddenly decreased. It was hardly by chance that

Some of the most sophisticated civilizations of the New World flourished in Central America. Center page, left: A votive statue made of jade and serpentine from the ancient Olmec civilization (1200–200 B.C.), and an Aztec warrior wearing the typical plumed headdress and black facial decorations.

The Inca Empire rose in South America. This was the most widespread civilization on the continent. Lower left: An aribal vase. This was a large vase, typical of the Incas, used for transporting liquids. (Painted clay, Pachacamac, A.D. fifteenth century)

the great pre-Columbian civilizations flourished in the zone between the Tropic of Cancer and the Tropic of Capricorn where the food was more plentiful.

The Pre-Columbian Civilizations

The most complex civilizations developed in Central America and in the Andes. Here rose highly-organized states, with monumental architecture and sculpture, together with state religions. In the southern part of Central America, and in Colombia, western Venezuela, and northern Ecuador, the civilizations were less sophisticated and were based primarily on agriculture. A similar pattern was evident in the Caribbean islands. Societies based on horticulture also developed in the Mississippi River area, while tribal societies – whose economies were based on the cultivation of manioc – were present to the east of the Andes, and in the Orinoco and Amazon river basins.

A large number of tribes that thrived on a mixed economy lived between the Atlantic coast of North America and the Great Lakes. The men of these tribes hunted game, while the women tilled the fields. Toward the west were the vast prairies, crossed by nomads in pursuit of bison, or buffalo. There are several theories regarding the origins of this type of Native American nomadic culture. It seems most likely that at the end of the seventeenth century, the tribes living on the edge of the prairies found themselves displaced by the advance of the European colonies on the one hand and by more powerful Indian tribes on the other. None of this would have been possible without the horse which. was brought to North America by the Spanish and spread rapidly throughout the continent.

The arid regions of the Far West of what is now the United States were home to smaller groups of Indians who lived by gathering roots. Meanwhile on the Pacific coast a culture dependent on fishing for its survival had developed.

In the Americas, in general, there were many types of cultures, and the continent had such varied physical and climactic conditions that life for the European settlers was a continuous adventure. For them it may truly be said that a "New World" had been discovered.

The lid of an Aztec urn in gilded terra-cotta, on which traces of red and yellow paint are evident. Right: A Mayan monument in stone, about 15 feet (4 meters) high, situated in Copán, Honduras, and dating from the eighth century.

Left: The Inca city of Machu Picchu today: Machu Picchu is a fine example of the monumental architecture created by the Incas.

An Inca warrior.

The illustrations show some of the pre-Columbian peoples living throughout North and South America.

Top left: An Ipiutak hunter. The Ipiutaks settled in the Arctic. The igloo was the typical nomadic dwelling of these Arctic people, who lived by hunting and fishing. A harpoon tip made from walrus tusk.

Top right: A warrior beside a typical dwelling of the Eastern Woodland Indians, one of the most numerous groups of Native Americans.

THE DISCOVERY OF AMERICA

The Relations Between Europe and the World

Throughout the Middle Ages, Europe had kept its links with Asia. The Mongol Empire (thirteenth – fourteenth centuries) in particular, had favored contacts between Europe and the Far East. Trade was by land over the Silk Route, which began in Asia Minor and led to China.

This profitable economic exchange was weakened with the rise of the Turkish Empire, which in the fifteenth century, extended from Asia Minor as far west as Egypt. This new Muslim power made it difficult for Europeans to reach India and China on the traditional overland trade routes. New routes had to be found. This search triggered a series of geographical discoveries that were aided greatly by new types of ships being built in Europe.

The New Vessels

The galley, a tall, wide vessel, was able to carry 200 to 300 tons of goods, but it was fragile and easy prey for pirates. Thus in Venice and Genoa another type of vessel was developed. It was enormous compared to the galley, tall and wide, with two or three decks, three masts, and a host of sails. This ship could resist both storms and pirates because it was a floating fortress. Moreover, since the ships were so large, it was no longer necessary to put into port so frequently. Spain, Flanders, or England could be reached directly from Genoa or Venice. In this way Italian, Spanish, and Portuguese sailors, and later all western European sailors, were able to learn the techniques of sailing on the high seas. These were essential skills for those wishing to risk voyages toward unknown lands. For these journeys of discovery, smaller vessels able to navigate along coasts and up rivers were used. Called caravels they were excellent sailing ships.

The First "Discoverers," The Vikings

The Vikings, a race of expert navigators, lived in Europe between the ninth and eleventh centuries. From Scandinavia, the Vikings sailed all the seas and rivers they found. Vikings settled in Iceland, which had been previously uninhabited, and ventured as far west as Greenland. From here, toward the end of the tenth century, they reached the coasts of Labrador and Newfoundland. The Vikings reached the North American continent, but they set up no regular links with Europe, and their colonies vanished.

Christopher Columbus

The reasons for the journeys to America in the fifteenth century may be found in the Europeans' desire to reach the riches of Asia, especially India and China, without having to cross Muslim territory. By this time many scholars knew that the earth was round and that it should be possible to reach Asia by sailing west across the Atlantic. The curiosity of the Spanish, Portuguese, and Italians, together with the burning desire to reach the fabulous riches of the East, sharpened the Europeans' courage.

Christopher Columbus, a sailor of outstanding courage and willpower, was born in Genoa in 1451. He moved to Portugal in 1476, where he learned Portuguese techniques of navigation. He visited Africa and England and in 1480 submitted to the Portuguese a plan to reach India or China by sailing toward the West. At this time the Portuguese were more interested in exploring Africa, and they rejected Columbus' proposal. He presented his plan to the French and English

The shortest route from Europe to the American continent, as shown on the map, was taken by the Vikings who reached the coasts of Labrador in the tenth century, but did not set up regular contacts.

Top of page: A typical Viking longship used for ocean crossings.

In 1492 Columbus left Spain for Asia. He landed instead on an island in the Bahamas, as shown on the map. The scene illustrates the arrival of Columbus' three caravels in the New World.

kings, but with the same result. He then tried the Spanish court of Ferdinand and Isabella, and finally obtained their consent. Ferdinand and Isabella named Columbus viceroy, admiral, and governor of all the lands he might discover.

Columbus set sail from Palos in August 1492. On October 12 he reached an island in the Bahamas that he named San Salvador. He began to explore the other islands in the archipelago, then sailing east, he touched Cuba and Hispaniola, where he left some members of his crew. On

March 15, 1493, he returned to Palos where his voyage had begun. This is how Columbus "discovered" America. However, he himself continued to believe he had reached eastern Asia.

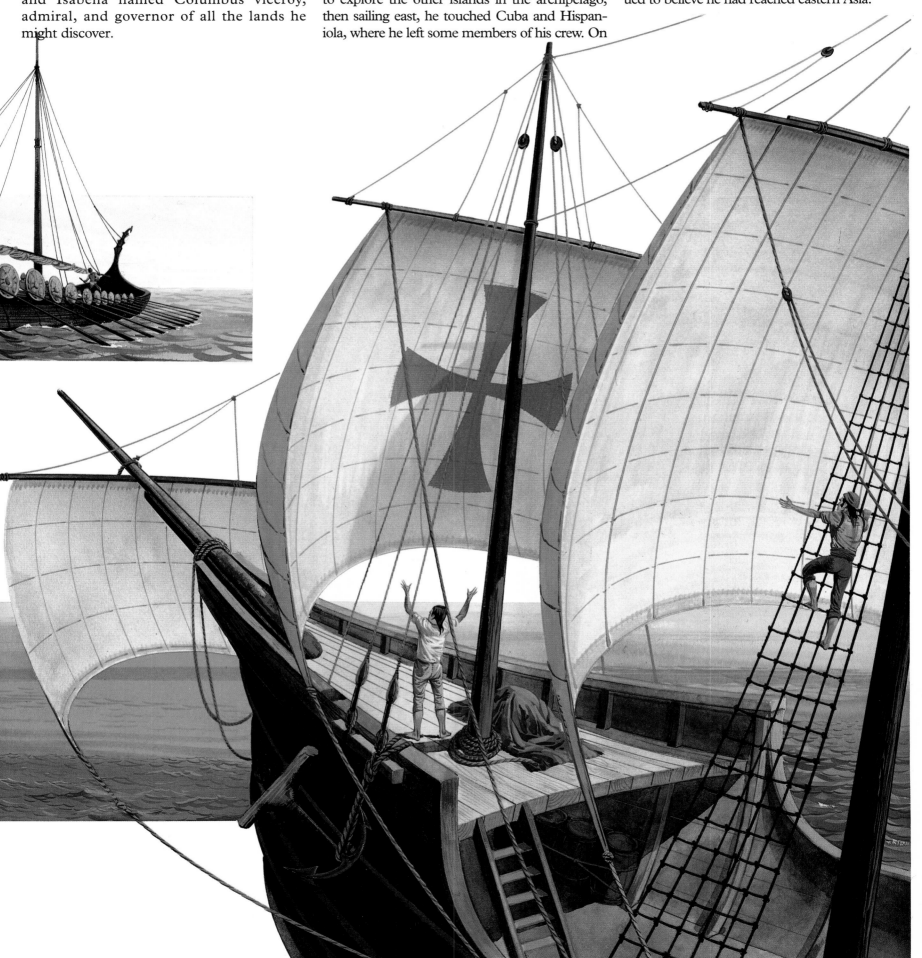

9

THE EARLY VOYAGES OF EXPLORATION

Western Europe was amazed and almost incredulous at the news of the "discovery" of a New World and accepted the idea slowly. For example, even twenty years after Columbus landed in America, mapmakers following Columbus' wishful thinking still insisted on denying the existence of the American continents and continued to draw maps on which the Americas were just a large appendage of Asia.

The vagueness and comparative lack of scientific precision of these times helps us understand both the shock felt by the western Europeans and the social climate at the time of the discovery. Christopher Columbus himself, who undertook another four voyages to the West Indies between 1492 and 1504, gave inexact or incorrect information about his findings. For example, he confused the plant aloe for agave, and turkeys for chickens. (Neither chickens nor aloe existed in America.) He was full of superstitious beliefs that provoked visions. He recorded having seen mermaids and men with tails. During his third voyage, in 1498, on reaching the mouth of the Orinoco River, he was convinced he had arrived in the Garden of Eden, a paradise on earth.

On the basis of these vague and often incorrect reports, the old world began to form an opinion of the new. In the West Indies the Europeans expected to find either a difficult life and death or an earthly paradise, filled with slaves, gold, and adventure. The first nucleus of conquerors set sail with these contrasting visions in mind.

The Later Voyages of Discovery

As soon as Columbus returned to Spain, Ferdinand and Isabella asked for his discoveries to be legally recognized. In 1493, the Spanish-born pope, Alexander VI, issued a papal bull, *Inter Caetera*. This document traced an imaginary line one hundred leagues (350 miles) west of the Azores and granted the Spanish sovereignty over all the lands that had been discovered together with those that would be discovered beyond it. However, the Portuguese monarchy asked for the revision of the document granted to the Spanish. In 1494 the Treaty of Tordesillas was drawn up. A new demarcation line separating the Spanish and Portuguese colonial empires was fixed, this time at a point roughly 1,295 miles (2,084 km) west of the Cape Verde Islands.

Between 1502 and 1512, the military exploration and domination of the Caribbean islands began. Nicolas de Ovando brought about the control of Hispaniola (Santo Domingo) from 1502 to 1508. In 1509 Juan de Esquivel

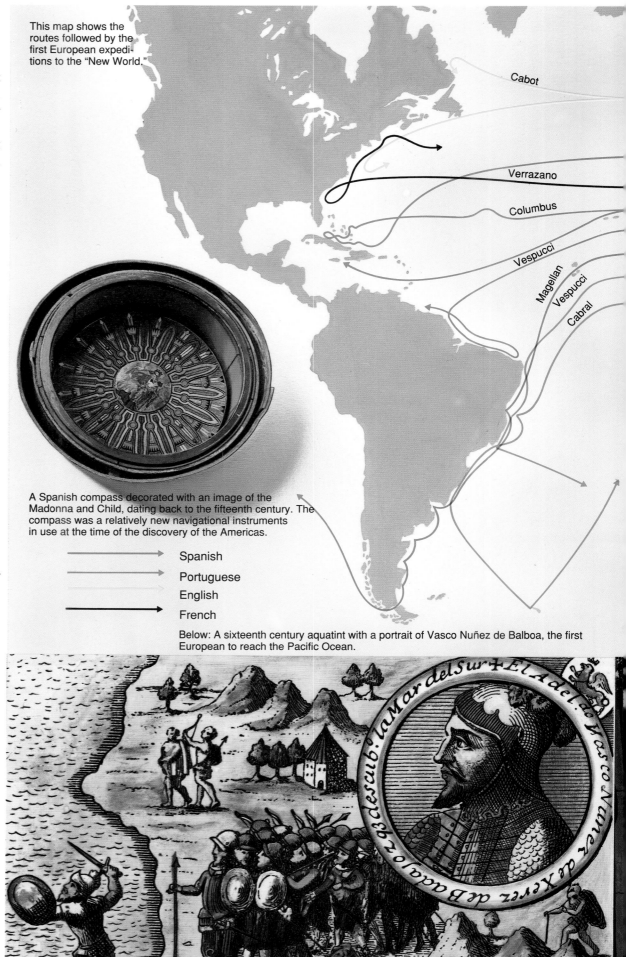

This map shows the routes followed by the first European expeditions to the "New World."

Cabot

Verrazano

Columbus

Vespucci

Magellan

Vespucci

Cabral

A Spanish compass decorated with an image of the Madonna and Child, dating back to the fifteenth century. The compass was a relatively new navigational instruments in use at the time of the discovery of the Americas.

Spanish

Portuguese

English

French

Below: A sixteenth century aquatint with a portrait of Vasco Nuñez de Balboa, the first European to reach the Pacific Ocean.

Vasco Nuñez toma posesion de la Mar del Sur

The New World according to an atlas printed in 1519.

colonized Jamaica. Between 1511 and 1514, Diego de Velasquez and Juan Ponce de Leon conquered Cuba and Puerto Rico.

The leaders of the exploration of the Isthmus of Panama and part of the inland regions of what is now northern Colombia were members of the group that had accompanied Columbus on his first voyage. From 1497 on, Vicente Yáñez Pinzón explored the South American coasts of the Caribbean Sea and then the coasts of Brazil as far as the Amazon River. The Isthmus of Panama and the coasts of Colombia were reached by Rodrigo de Bastidas in 1500, Juan de la Cosa in 1504, and Alonso de Ojeda in 1508, and in 1513, Vasco Nuñez de Balboa, after an exhausting twenty-day trek through swamps, forests, mountains, mud, and torrential rain, became the first European to cross the Isthmus of Panama and reach the Pacific Ocean.

Between 1499 and 1502, the Florentine Amerigo Vespucci, explored part of the South American coast. The reports of his voyage did much to enlighten the western Europeans about the new continent, which could no longer be confused with Asia. From about 1507 on, the continent became known as America.

In 1500 the Portuguese navigator Pedro Cabral landed in Brazil, while the Florentine Giovanni Caboto, better known as John Cabot, representing the English Crown, reached the North American continent in 1497. He was followed by Giovanni da Verrazano and Jacques Cartier, both in the service of the French Crown. In 1519 the expedition led by Portuguese Ferdinand Magellan, sailing for Spain, completed the first circumnavigation of the globe. Magellan did not finish the trip, for he was killed in the Philippines.

In 1544 Francesco de Orellana explored the continent along the Marañón River – the Amazon. Then between 1540 and 1554, Pedro de Valdivia explored Chile.

Europe and the Planet

With the discovery and the conquest of the Americas, Europe, the globe's smallest continent, began to establish worldwide contacts. The center of economic gravity shifted gradually from the European seas – the North, the Baltic, and the Mediterranean – to the Atlantic and Pacific Oceans.

World commerce increased enormously with the importation of overseas products, such as potatoes, corn, tobacco, and sugarcane. Politically speaking, the period of the exploration of the New World marked the rise of Spain and Portugal as nation-states, followed later by the Netherlands, France, and England. The expansion of worldwide European influence began with the exploration and conquest of America.

Cortés landed near what is now Veracruz, Mexico, in 1519. In general, the Spanish were welcomed by the natives. Several believed the white men were gods who came from the sea.

Central America at the Time of the Discoveries with the Routes of Columbus and Cortés.

Cuba

Caribbean Sea

Aztec Empire

Mayas

Cortés 1519–1525
Columbus 1492–1493
Columbus 1502–1504

The conquistadors destroying the Aztec idols in the Temple of Cempoala, where human sacrifices were performed.

According to native legends, the coming of the Spanish was announced by a fatal omen, the passage of a comet.

A cinerary urn used to hold human ashes, with the effigy of the goddess of water. (*Mayan Temple Museum, Mexico City*)

THE AGE OF THE CONQUISTADORS: MEXICO AND CENTRAL AMERICA

The Aztecs and Their Predecessors

At the beginning of the sixteenth century when the Spanish invaded Mexico, the Aztecs ruled over a powerful empire. They had access to the Pacific and Atlantic oceans and controlled the main lines of communication in Central America. Backed by a powerful army, the Aztecs had been able to become masters of the region rapidly, and they ruled their empire from their capital, Tenochtitlán, now the site of Mexico City.

The empire was subdivided into administrative regions, each of which contributed taxes. The Aztec civilization developed an intensive system of agriculture, constructed many impressive buildings and temples, and formulated simple but exact theories of astronomy and a system of writing. Their writing was not phonetic, but based on pictograms. Much importance was placed on religion, above all on the worship of the sun. Human sacrifice was a widespread practice.

Aztec society was rigid and static which, in part, explains the ease with which it was overthrown by the Spanish. The social structure included the Lord of Men (the king), the nobility, the powerful priest class, the merchants, the artisans, the peasant farmers, and finally the slaves. Cortés conquered this powerful empire with the help of six hundred soldiers, sixteen horses, ten cannons, and thirteen arquebuses – an early form of musket.

The Conquistadors' Mentality

In Spanish history, 1492 was not only the year of the discovery of America. It was also the year that Granada, the last area of Muslim resistance in Spain, was conquered. This event marked the end of the Reconquista period of Spanish history, a period during which Christian Spanish forces reconquered Spain and brought the Muslim dominance of the area to its end.

The new monarchs ruling Spain were Ferdinand of Aragón and Isabella of Castile. They had managed to unite the members of Spanish society under the Crown. They put an end to the struggles between the nobles, who were granted important privileges for supporting the government of the kingdom.

The men who took part in the conquest of America came from all levels of society, but they all had one common wish – to find overseas the fortunes they lacked at home. Among these men were poorer nobles who had taken part in the Reconquista process, but who, at its end, had found themselves with few opportunities. Several of these aristocrats had been ruined by the economic crisis that had hit Spain during the years immediately before the discovery of the Americas. It was not by chance that both Cortés and Pizarro came from Estremadura, one of the poorest regions of Spain.

For these men, the departure for America meant an opportunity to become rich and to perform heroic deeds, and it is not strange that little is known of their lives before the "American" period.

Cortés Conquest of Mexico

Hernán Cortés, born in 1485, landed in Santo Domingo in 1504. After a rather disappointing initial period on Santo Domingo, he became secretary to the governor of Cuba and in 1511 took part in the war to check a revolt there. In this fashion he gained considerable experience in the tactical and strategic methods for successfully fighting the native population.

In 1519 Cortés left Cuba for Mexico. This marked the beginning of a new phase of the Spanish presence in Central America, which was concluded by the submission of the amazing empire dominated by Moctezuma, lord of the Aztecs. In April 1519, Cortés landed in a flat area that appeared easy to capture and to settle. Here he established the settlement of Veracruz as the base for his explorations. In general, he was accepted by the people, who thought he could help free them from the tyranny of the Aztecs. Cortés soon realized the resentment these people felt for the Aztecs, who even demanded they supply human sacrifices for their religious ceremonies. The Spaniard took advantage of the situation and convinced a number of these peoples to join him in overthrowing the Aztecs.

Cortés' next step was to use his superior weapons in a strategic way. The Aztecs were familiar neither with gunpowder nor horses. To better understand Cortés' relatively rapid conquest of Mexico, it is important to understand the skill with which he used the weapons he had with him. He ordered his men to shoot their firearms in unison, to destroy trees and hillsides with their cannons, and to make the greatest amount of noise possible. In this way he was able to terrify and confuse a large army. Cortés' venture ended in 1521 with the destruction of the Aztec capital and the massacre of its inhabitants.

For the next twenty years, the conquistadors continued their conquest of Central America. They also subdued other peoples, like the Mayas, and explored farther south to the lesser known territories of Guatemala and Honduras.

THE AGE OF THE CONQUISTADORS: THE ANDES REGION

The region of the northern Andes, in present-day Colombia, was the original center of the Chibcha people. They had ventured south as far as modern-day Ecuador, and north beyond the Isthmus of Panama as far as Nicaragua. The most developed regions were the Cauca River valley and the Bogotá Plateau, both in present-day Colombia. Governing power was in the hands of despotic chiefs. In the Cauca River valley the people lived in small tribal groups, each headed by a lord. The Chibcha lived in villages. Their economy was based on agriculture.

To the south, the Inca Empire was the most powerful in ancient America. It was known as "the kingdom of the four points of the compass" – a kingdom that had no bounds. The Incas originated from the city of Cuzco, high on the Andean plateau. The spread of the Inca civilization began in the first half of the fifteenth century. Several nearby tribes asked for help from their powerful neighbor and soon found themselves absorbed into the kingdom of the Inca, the Lord of Cuzco. The Incas extended their rule over the entire region of the Andes, as far as central Ecuador. The Inca emperor, Tupac Yupanqui (1471–1493), conquered what we now call Bolivia and ventured into Chile, and northwest Argentina. Tupac's successor, Huayna Capac (1493–1527), pressed north, beyond present-day Quito. The empire extended as far north as the present-day southern frontier of Colombia and took in Ecuador, Peru, and the Bolivian region of the Andes and Argentina, extending as far south as the Maule River in central Chile.

Pizarro and the Conquest of Peru

Francisco Pizarro arrived in America in 1502. His military skills soon became apparent, and he took part in various missions against natives. He was illiterate, which partly

explains why there are fewer written records of the conquest of Peru than there are for the conquest of Mexico.

The contact between the Spanish and the Inca Empire was different than the contact between the Spanish and the Central American civilizations. This time there was no surprise at finding sophisticated forms of civilization. There were, however, fresh challenges, due to the sheer size of the empire.

Before its conquest, Peru was the object of myths, legends, and stories built around the various attempts at its exploration. Pizarro was obsessed with the idea of its conquest, but his first expedition (1524) was a total failure. Two years later he undertook a second voyage and in January 1527 reached Tumbes, a city overlooking the Gulf of Guayaquil, on the border between Peru and present-day Ecuador. The city was inhabited by an extremely civilized people, only too eager to exchange gifts with the small group of Spaniards. Pizarro received objects of gold and silver, textiles, and ceramics.

He was informed that the Inca Huayna Capac had died in 1527, and that his two sons, Huascar, who lived in Cuzco, and Atahualpa, who lived in Quito, challenged each other for the throne. Pizarro decided to try a third, and, he hoped, decisive expedition. He became involved in the Inca civil war (1531). In the battle of Cuzco, Atahualpa took his brother prisoner. The Spaniards first supported Atahualpa, but later took him prisoner and eventually killed him in 1533. After the death of the sovereign, the Inca Empire disintegrated.

By 1539, the Spanish controlled the empire, even though resistance continued until 1572, when the last Inca leader, Tupac Amaru, was killed by the Spanish. Peru attracted many opportunists, and its treasures held an irresistible fascination for the Spanish adventurers. They struggled among themselves to obtain the greatest quantity of the spoils of the conquest. These rivalries often led to civil wars, and Pizarro himself was killed on one such occasion. These internal conflicts between the Spanish prolonged the conquest and presented an extremely bad example of Spanish power to the natives. The reaction of the Spanish government was to send troops to deal with the rebels and put an end to these civil wars in 1542.

The scene shows a meeting between Spanish soldiers and the Incas. The children are curious about the horse. The horse was introduced to the American continents by the Spanish. Before the arrival of the Europeans, llamas were used to transport goods in Andean lands. The Inca Empire (1438-1532), in particular, organized caravans of goods carried by llamas. The goods were left at a building that served as a relay station and warehouse, as shown in the picture. In the background, the circular terraced hillsides used by the Incas can be seen. This ingenious method of farming helped to develop a system of agriculture that could support a large population.

A hat typical of the Andes region.

In this ancient Inca drawing, the peasant farmers are using a foot plow to prepare the land for sowing.

A traditional handloom. These looms were easily transportable and the upper edge could be easily fixed to any vertical support.

The handle of a blade representing a god of the heavens or of the moon. The figure was inlaid and painted, then beads and filigree were added. This object comes from the northern coast of Peru and is an example of the fine art produced by the Inca goldsmiths.

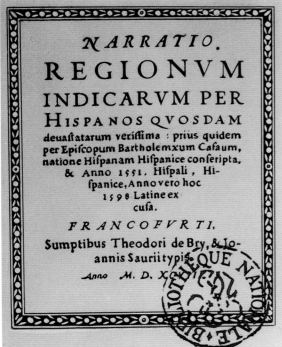

NARRATIO.
REGIONVM
INDICARVM PER
HISPANOS QVOSDAM
deuaſtatarum veriſſima : prius quidem
per Epiſcopum Bartholemxum Caſaum,
natione Hiſpanam Hiſpanice conſcripta,
& Anno 1551. Hiſpali , Hiſpanice, Anno vero hoc
1598 Latine ex
cuſa.
FRANCOFVRTI,
Sumptibus Theodori de Bry, & Io-
annis Saurii typis.
Anno M. D. XC.

TREATMENT OF NATIVE AMERICANS

The Tragedy of the Conquered

The arrival of the Spanish and their subsequent conquests were traumatic experiences for the natives of Central and South America. The Indian version of the conquest is recorded in only a fragmentary manner. Some Native Americans enlisted the help of some of the more understanding Spaniards, others learned the Latin alphabet after the conquest and used it to preserve the memory of the destruction of their people. Every report, chronicle, elegy, or story is full of feelings of insecurity, misery, and a progressively somber sense of resignation.

According to scholars, the decimation of the native population of Central and South America in the sixteenth century varied from between 60 percent and 90 percent. The con-

quistadors' behavior toward the Indians was one of unprecedented cruelty. The Spanish assaulted villages and cities. They hanged, quartered, mutilated, and burned alive men, women, and children. The horror did not end there. Out of sheer desperation, to avoid falling live into Spanish hands, many natives actually hanged themselves or took poison, and there were many cases of mass suicide. If the tribes attempted to revolt, they were massacred.

Apart from being eliminated by physical violence, the Indian populations were crushed by forced removal from their homes and heavy labor, for which they were totally unprepared. They were defeated not only in a military, social, cultural, and psychological fashion, but they also suffered greatly from their lack of immunity to European diseases. Epidemics of

smallpox were a real scourge. Even measles, aggravated by exposure to the sun and by the habit of seeking relief by taking cold baths, claimed numerous victims. Many natives died of simple influenza, which degenerated into a fatal condition from lack of care. The Spanish, on the other hand, if in much smaller numbers, were plagued by rheumatic fevers and malaria.

Bartolomé de Las Casas: The Apostle of the Indies

Bartolomé de Las Casas arrived in Santo Domingo in 1502. In the beginning, he lived like all the other Spaniards, enjoying the comfortable life that resulted from exploiting the natives. In 1511 he had a deep crisis of conscience and, the following year, he became a Roman Catholic priest. He then dedicated himself to defending

the Indians' rights. In his work *A Short Account of the Destruction of the Indies,* published in 1552, he described the horrors of the conquest and attacked those who regarded the Indians as inferior beings. Just before his death in 1566, he wrote *The History of the Indies,* in which he recognized the value of the pre-Columbian civilizations. Sadly, despite his good intentions, by the time his writings became widely known, it was too late. The Native Americans had already been subjugated or annihilated.

The Roman Catholic Church's Attitude Toward the Americas

The discovery of America had a considerable effect on the field of theology and religion. Christian Europe was surprised, confused, and unprepared when faced with the existence of Native Americans. The sacred scriptures clearly stated that the voice of God had arrived everywhere. Saint Paul's Epistle to the Romans stressed that there were no people who had not heard the Word of Christ. But then who were these "Indios," these peoples who were ignorant of the Word of Christ? What was to be done with them? They could be converted with patience, or by force, or they could be treated like animals lacking any form of rationality.

Those who supported the theory of conversion to Christianity without the use of force attempted to slow down and reduce the fury of the soldiers. They appealed to the Spanish monarchs and to the pope for help. The spread of Protestantism in seventeenth century Europe actually stimulated conversion of the Indians to a certain extent. Roman Catholicism, under pressure in Europe due to the Protestants, could now find new strength in America. But some priests and missionaries who accompanied the conquistadors took part directly in the destruction, plunder, and exploitation of the Indians.

The Conversion of the Indians

The sudden discovery of countless souls who had never heard of Christ represented a challenge for the Roman Catholic church and for the Spanish Crown. The work of conversion was extremely difficult and could only be entrusted to missionaries who were free from worldly ambitions. The church and the Crown found the most suitable monks in the Franciscan, Dominican, and Augustinian orders, together with the Order of Mercy. These orders had in common both wide experience preaching to the poorer classes and highly disciplined organizations.

The first friars to reach the Americas had no precise program for converting the Indians and had to overcome numerous obstacles. The Native Americans inhabited a vast territory and did not understand Spanish, and, of course, none of the missionaries knew any of the local languages. The enormous task on hand forced the friars to use hasty methods in the beginning. Later the monks set up more organized Indian communities. In this way, the missionaries hoped to facilitate the conversion process and teach the Indians better methods of cultivating the land.

Converting the Indians proved much more difficult than they had imagined. The Indians were baptized and given religious instruction, but it is difficult to say how many were really Christian. Even those who witnessed the process had differing opinions on the subject. The Jesuits, for example, who arrived in America somewhat later than the early missionaries, were convinced that the Indians were Christians only in appearance and professed the faith only for fear of punishment. It is likely that the Indians adopted the rites and teachings that were nearest to their spiritual needs and to their way of life. In this way, a type of Christian religion was formed in which ele-

The Spanish took only a relatively short period of time to consolidate their empire due to the speed with which the settlers began to exploit the lands they had conquered. The Spanish created a highly bureaucratic dominion where full-time government officials administered a system centered on the orders of the Spanish monarchs. This system was able to guarantee increasing obedience of the laws.

The chief unit of government in Spanish America was the viceroyalty. In 1535 the Viceroyalty of New Spain was created and took in all the territories north of Panama. In 1542 the Viceroyalty of Peru was created, and it covered all the lands south of the Isthmus of Panama except for the coast of Venezuela.

The founding and development of urban centers was a typical feature of Spanish American colonization. City life was typical of the Spanish way of life and allowed the Crown more control over the colonies.

This scene shows the port of Havana, Cuba, one of the main centers of intercontinental trade. Colonial goods, such as tobacco, sugar, cotton, lumber, and silver, left this port for Spain. Goods from Spain would arrive here and then be distributed to other Spanish American centers. In this region of the New World, the Native American population were soon replaced by slaves from Africa who were imported to perform the hardest work.

THE FIRST SPANISH CENTERS OF COLONIZATION IN THE AMERICAS

Under the Control of Spain

The exploration and conquest of American territory was accompanied by a slow but constant build-up of a governmental bureaucracy. Spain never delegated its sovereignty over the new lands to anyone. In the beginning, however, it granted the rights to the exploration, the occupation, and the administration of the territories to private individuals. Naturally, the first obstacle to an efficient form of control was the length of the voyage between Spain and the new territories. Ships took about sixty days to reach the Caribbean islands from Cadíz, Spain, and eighty to one hundred days for the return trip. It was therefore easy for the few thousand Spanish present in the new territories to avoid total obedience to any orders from Spain.

Spain, however, showed immediate interest in the development of the American lands. In 1503 the Casa de Contratación was founded in Seville. This organization was responsible for drawing up lists of passengers, goods, and contracts for exploration. The Casa was charged with checking on and organizing emigration to the Americas. Anyone who wished to go had to have the approval of this organization.

Individuals and families emigrated to the Americas for different reasons: to make their fortune, to improve their social position, to escape justice, to serve God as missionaries, to serve the king as officers, or to accompany or find a husband. The Crown, in fact, encouraged the emigration of women because it considered the Christian family the basis of the type of society it wished to create in the New World. Between 1540 and 1579, artisans, tradespeople, missionaries, and government officials began to emigrate to the Americas. In 1511 the Council of the Indies was created to help the Spanish Crown administer the new possessions. The treasurers, accountants, and councillors set to work to oversee the activities of the conquistadors and to look after the interests of the Crown.

The "Encomiendas"

The social development in the Spanish possessions in the Americas was soon founded on the system of the *encomiendas*. In Spain, the *encomienda* existed in towns, villages, and monasteries under the dominion of the Crown. The monarch assigned the administration of a certain amount of land to a deserving person for a fixed period of time. The assignee had the right to collect taxes for the Crown from anyone living on the land and to request the inhabitants to carry out the work necessary to ensure the *encomienda* was efficiently run. The concession was temporary and the land remained the property of the Crown. The same type of system developed in the Americas. Through the *encomienda*, the beneficiary collected for his own use a large proportion of the taxes the Indians should have been paying to the Spanish government. The taxes were both in the form of money or goods. Often the Indians were too poor to pay and were thus forced to work free for the *encomendero*, who was supposed to give them protection and instruction in return.

In reality, this system of the *encomiendas* in America degenerated into a system of slavery. The regime was soon condemned by the church and was subject to ever increasing controls from Spain. The condemnation of clergy like de Las Casas was accompanied by the concern of the Crown, which wanted to avoid the creation of a Spanish American aristocracy at all costs. In 1512 the Laws of Burgos condemned the slavery of Indians, but the laws were never enforced.

Urban Centers

A typical feature of Spanish colonization was the creation of urban centers. Fortified towns offered better defense and facilitated communication. But the founding of towns and cities corresponded above all to the Spanish way of life and the desire of Spain to keep the colonies under better control.

The building of urban centers began on Hispaniola in 1501. The king requested Governor Nicolas de Ovando to create a city on the island. Ovando built San Domingo. The city had straight streets that crossed each other at right angles, modeled on the way in which Spanish cities were built during the Middle Ages. The Spanish government rapidly issued general rules for the construction of urban centers in the Americas. The plan of the city would be like a chessboard: squares, streets, and blocks of houses had to be built in straight lines. The point of departure would be the central square, and the street system would develop from this point. This type of town planning became typical of the Spanish American cities. Despite state orders, however, many colonies spread into the surrounding countryside, and, at the end of the colonial era, there were more Spanish living in the countryside than in cities.

THE EUROPEANS' USE OF THE ROUTES ACROSS THE ATLANTIC

Throughout the entire sixteenth century, the French, the Dutch, and the English explored North America and established settlements there. By the end of the century, these nations had become very powerful. Their economies had growing needs for raw materials, and merchants gained an increasing amount of influence within the various governments. The settlements on the American continents provided furs, dyes, animal skins, plantation crops, and sometimes precious metals.

During the seventeenth century, Holland became a shipbuilding center. The Dutch vessels were fast, agile, and well suited to dealing with piracy. The Dutch also were such good constructors of warships that foreign powers made increasing use of their services. The naval power of the northern European nations had grown to rival that of Spain and Portugal.

Despite the improvement in navigational techniques, life on board ship during the long ocean crossings still remained very hard. The daily tasks the sailors had to perform were often dangerous, and sickness, in particular scurvy, claimed many victims among the crews. The living conditions often drove them to mutiny against their captains, a crime that carried the death penalty.

In the sixteenth century, some European countries, such as England, began to penetrate American waters. Fast ships made frequent attacks on the Spanish domains in the Caribbean Sea and along the Brazilian coast. Ships regularly attacked convoys of Spanish merchant ships heading for Europe. Their favorite targets were the Spanish galleons carrying gold and other precious metals extracted from American mines. The Spanish viewed these attacks as outright acts of piracy, which many of them were.

The on-going dispute in Europe between the Spanish king Philip II and the English queen Elizabeth I took place on the oceans to the

A sextant is a navigational instrument still used today to determine longitude and latitude.

Together with the compass, the astrolabe, such as the one shown here, allowed sailors to identify a ship's position thus making the voyage safer.

detriment of the Spanish trade with the colonies. This undeclared war guaranteed considerable gains for the English Crown. English privateers were not officially at the service of the queen. They were their own masters, merchant adventurers, who risked their skins and supported the consequences of their actions alone. If their actions provoked embarrassment, the English government repudiated them. If, instead, the attacks on the Spanish galleons met with success, the booty was shared with the queen. The penetration into the Americas was thus more the result of the enterprising spirit of audacious privateers, rather than the initiative of the Crown. Thanks to them, England crippled Spain's merchant fleet in a relatively short time.

The Legal Justifications

The privateers did not always limit their efforts to merchant shipping. Their captains were often able explorers. Sir Francis Drake, for example, circumnavigated the globe in three years (1577–1580).

From the beginning, the northern European approach to the colonization of the Americas differed radically from the Spanish occupation. The extensive Spanish Empire was conquered through greed, the quest for adventure, and the missionaries' desire to convert the Indians to Roman Catholicism. But it was also the result of a notable administrative effort. The establishment of the power of the Spanish Crown in the Americas began almost immediately after Columbus' first journey. Nothing similar was ever set up by the northern Europeans in their American dominions. The Dutch, for example, were primarily interested in founding trading posts, and consequently, no central power interfered in the administration of these American possessions.

In the English dominions, the authority of the Crown and of Parliament was very superficial and rarely managed, or desired, to control the political life of the colonies. These initial differences had a lasting influence on later stages of the history of the United States.

The illustration on the left shows a naval shipyard in Holland. In the seventeenth century, Holland became the center for shipbuilding. The Dutch vessels were fast and well suited to the long ocean crossings. The Dutch also became the best builders of warships, and foreign powers made use of Dutch techniques and experience when building their own fleets of warships.

The illustration on this page shows ships of the Dutch West Indies Company. For the most part, the company did not establish many permanent colonies in the Americas, but preferred setting up trading posts along the coasts.

THE PORTUGUESE IN AMERICA

Portuguese Expansion in Africa and Asia

Portuguese expansion, supported directly by the Crown, began in 1415 with the conquest of Ceuta, Morocco. The Portuguese thus hoped to secure direct access to the riches of Africa south of the Sahara. Up to this time, the Arabs had acted as intermediaries for the commerce of gold, spices, ivory, and slaves. After the capture of Ceuta, the Portuguese began to explore the west coast of Africa, where they soon set up trading posts for the collection of gold, ivory, and slaves. They established colonies based on the cultivation of sugarcane on the Atlantic islands of Madeira, the Azores, and Cape Verde.

In 1498 the Portuguese reached India by sea. They also took control of the Indian Ocean from the various Indian and Muslim principalities and kept control despite frequent attacks from the Turks. This supremacy was made possible by the construction of ports defended by stone fortresses. The most important of these bases was Goa in India. The majority of the local states were forced to pay taxes and sell their products to the Portuguese at fixed prices. Moreover, all trade conducted by non-Portuguese was subject to taxation. The Portuguese eventually continued their Far Eastern explorations as far as Indonesia, China, and Japan.

Map of Bahia, drawn around 1616. Bahia was the first capital of Brazil.

Above: The port of Lisbon in the sixteenth century, taken from an illustration of the time. Lisbon, together with Amsterdam in the Netherlands, was then a center of extensive trade with Africa and the Americas.

Portuguese Colonies in America

In 1500 the Portuguese explorer Pedro Cabral claimed the land now known as Brazil for Portugal. Compared to the riches discovered by the Spanish in Mexico and Peru, Brazil was a disappointment. It remained a third-rate colony for a long time, exploited primarily for its high quality lumber. The first Portuguese settlements were thus no more than simple trading posts. Only in 1534 did the Portuguese king John III decide to seriously colonize Brazil. He divided his American dominions into captaincies. Each consisted of a strip of coastline suitable for establishing a port plus an amount of territory stretching from the coast into the interior. These areas were assigned to those willing to commit themselves to colonize them at their own expense. In return for colonizing these areas, the settlers received ample economic and political rights within the area. In the political sense, the leader of the colony obtained the title of governor and captain and was allowed to govern his territory without interference from the king's officials. He also had the right to establish new towns and cities and to administer justice. In addition, there was a grant of economic privileges. He was exempt from paying taxes, and a fifth of the territory became his personal property. The remainder belonged to the Crown, but the governor-captain could divide this land among his followers.

Two obstacles to this type of colonization were the hostility of the natives, whom the Portuguese tried to reduce to slavery, and the ungovernable masses of Portuguese immigrants. Many of the latter were exiled criminals.

The Governor-General and Portuguese Emigration

The difficulties encountered in the attempts by the immigrants at colonization convinced the king to reinforce his administration in Brazil. A royal settlement office was founded from which the governor was expected to coordinate the activity of the captaincies conceded to private individuals. The royal office was established in Bahia, which became the first capital of Brazil. After 1565, the second royal office was founded in Rio de Janeiro.

The state did not check or control immigration to the American colonies. There was an early policy of forced emigration for criminals and rebellious nobles. Colonial governors had difficulty in keeping these exiles under control. In Portugal, the peasant class was not driven to emigrate because of a scarcity of land. On the contrary, there was a lack of labor. Many of the immigrants were impoverished aristocrats who emigrated to Brazil, together with their retinue of servants and farm workers. They came with the intention of creating huge plantations for the cultivation of sugarcane or cotton. When the first governor-general was selected, a law was introduced prohibiting the creation of vast estates. However, the law was not enforced, and the estates reached colossal proportions, especially in the northern provinces.

Regarding the immigration of foreigners to their colonies, the Portuguese laws were much less restrictive than the Spanish ones. Any Jew who had converted and been baptized was allowed to settle in Brazil. Foreigners were granted freedom of trade and other privileges. It was only at the time of the union between the Spanish and Portuguese crowns, 1580–1640, that Brazil closed its doors to foreigners.

Left: A boundary stone marking the Brazilian possessions of the king of Portugal (sixteenth century). Compared with the riches found by the Spanish in Mexico and Peru, Brazil seemed disappointing. The first Portuguese settlements were therefore simple trading posts.

Slaves working in a Brazilian sugar refinery. Despite the opposition of the Crown, vast estates developed in Brazil, where sugarcane and cotton were grown. African slaves provided the labor. Portuguese merchants were by far the most active in the slave trade.

Below: The Church of Saints Cosma and Damiano of Igaragu in Pernambuco was the first Brazilian church.

FRENCH SETTLEMENTS IN THE AMERICAS

The Antilles (West Indies)

In 1628 the French joined the English in settling the island of St. Christopher in the West Indies. Colonists cultivated tobacco and sugarcane, products which were highly appreciated and therefore much in demand in Europe. The French went on to colonize Martinique and Guadeloupe in 1635 and part of Santo Domingo in 1655.

The French islands became prosperous rapidly and were soon part of a system of international trade. The French bought slaves in Africa, sold them in the West Indies for African slave labor on the sugar and tobacco plantations, and exported the coveted colonial products to Europe. With the profits, the colonists were able to buy manufactured goods in Europe.

The relationship between the colonies and France was, however, not easy. Under Jean Baptiste Colbert, finance minister in the government of Louis XIV (1643–1715), there was a system of rigid state control of the economy, according to the principles of mercantilism. This doctrine declared that a nation should establish colonies to provide the raw materials it lacked and to serve as markets for the manufactured goods it produced. In this way, money would circulate between the nation and its colonies and would not enrich rival powers.

Colbert declared that colonial products should be exported only to France and that only goods made in France should be imported by the colonies. Thus, the colonies were no longer free to sell their products to the highest bidder or to buy goods at the cheapest price. To escape France's rigid economic policy, the French colonists living in the West Indies resorted to smuggling and organized several revolts against France.

New France

The French had begun to explore North America around 1541, when Jacques Cartier landed in Canada. In 1608 Samuel de Champlain founded a successful colony in Quebec and created a settlement at Montreal. From here the French pushed south to reach the Great Lakes' region and the Hudson River. From 1670 to 1685, due to the initiative of the fur traders, missionaries, and adventurers, New France expanded to include the region along the Mississippi River south to its delta.

From the time of Louis XIV, France tried to gain more profits from its North American territories, which lay between those belonging to Spain and those belonging to England. But France's interest in them remained sporadic, and the French living in North America often had the impression of being abandoned to their destiny. The areas settled by the French proved poor in precious metals, and in the case of Canada, were unable to produce the tropical products of sugar and tobacco so popular with the European market. Furs from this area were the main type of goods in demand in Europe.

America continued to be a distant land for the French, and only about sixty thousand colonists emigrated to the New World. Farm laborers, orphans, and soldiers chosen to defend French territories abroad were the most frequent emigrants to the North American continent.

French Louisiana

The entire Mississippi River basin was claimed for France in 1682 by the explorer Robert de LaSalle and named Louisiana in honor of the French king. The first stable French settlement in the area began in 1699, when Pierre le Moyne founded the colony of Biloxi in what is now the state of Mississippi. At the beginning of the eighteenth century, the principal settlement moved to Mobile, in what is now Alabama.

For almost fifty years, the political life of Louisiana was dominated by le Moyne, who was nicknamed the father of Louisiana. He was governor several times, and in 1718 he founded the city of New Orleans. The city became the capital of Louisiana in 1722. Relatively few Europeans settled in the French region of North America. In 1750, when the English colonies boasted one and a half million inhabitants, the French population had reached only around eighty thousand.

The French in South America

As early as 1504, several French ships appeared off the Brazilian coast and attacked Portuguese trading posts. Between 1520 and 1530, the French became more aggressive and their actions caused considerable damage to the Portuguese settlements. However, with the exception of French Guiana, the French presence in South America never developed into permanent settlements.

Clockwise from the left: The open-air trading center in Quebec, Canada. On market days Native Americans came to the center to exchange goods with the French. In return for beaver skins, the Indians received hats, glass beads, and metal goods.

This illustration shows slaves being sold in a market in the French Antilles. The French made huge profits from the slave trade. Slaves captured by French merchants in Africa were sold to colonists in the Antilles. The African slaves labored in the sugar and cotton plantations of the West Indies.

A tobacco manufacturer in France. Tobacco, together with sugar and cotton, was one of the chief products imported to France from its American possessions.

DUTCH NAVAL AND COMMERCIAL POWER

The Development of a New Colonial Power

During the first half of the seventeenth century, the Dutch managed to create a vast trade network that extended throughout the world. They overwhelmed the competition with their large ships that were able to transport the most varied cargoes. Whatever and wherever goods had to be carried, from the more traditional products, like pepper, to the new products from both the North and South American colonies, like sugar, tea, coffee, and rum, the Dutch were present. Their fleets made up 80 percent of all European merchant shipping.

In 1602 a certain number of Dutch trading companies merged together to form a single company – The Dutch East India Company. This organization was entirely the result of the initiative of the Dutch middle class. It was an enterprise created by merchants, operating as a local company able to make use of the amazingly energetic and practical qualities of its members. While the Dutch lived in sumptuous houses, they maintained a sober and thrifty life-style. They had a well-developed social system and supported schools, charitable institutions, and orphanages.

The policy of commercial expansion went hand in hand with the undermining of Portuguese competition. Little by little, the Dutch managed to obtain the monopoly of the traffic in the region of Southeast Asia. The Dutch toppled the Portuguese but imitated their style. Instead of penetrating into the territories and establishing real colonial settlements, as the Spanish did, the Dutch, for the most part, built trading posts on the coasts of Asia, Africa, and the Americas. Exceptions to this policy were the colony founded in 1619 in Indonesia, around Batavia (present-day Djakarta), the permanent settlement of a group of colonists in 1652 near the Cape of Good Hope, and the founding of New Amsterdam (now New York City) in 1623. The trading activities of the Dutch merchants were accompanied by intense geographic exploration, which led to the exploration of the Australian coasts among others.

The vast commercial traffic organized by the Dutch East India Company was controlled from Amsterdam, which became the intermediary point between the most distant markets. From Amsterdam, it was possible to obtain a global impression of the volume of worldwide supply and demand.

The Dutch in America

The first Dutch expeditions set out for the Americas in the sixteenth century. The consequences of the political rivalry with Spain were also felt overseas. Between 1580 and 1640, privateers from the Dutch West Indies Company attacked the Spanish Silver Fleet. These ships transported the precious metals mined in the Americas across the ocean to Spain.

The Portuguese colonial empire in South America suffered, too, from Dutch competition. By 1630 the Dutch had captured the city of Bahia and six captaincies in Brazil. These territories were important for the exploitation of Brazil's sugarcane and coffee, and for the slave trade. Recife became the chief Dutch base for the defense of the northeastern coasts of South America, but the city was recaptured by the Portuguese in 1654. The Dutch also conquered Curaçao in 1634 and Guiana (now Surinam) in 1636.

In 1609, the Englishman Henry Hudson, in the service of the Dutch, crossed the Atlantic Ocean hoping to find a much searched for passage through the North American continent that would lead to China. Hudson sailed up part of a river hoping it would be the northwest passage. It was not, but eventually the river would be named for him. Hudson's journey proved fortunate. In 1623 the Dutch decided to settle the area that appeared inviting and worth colonizing. In particular, they settled on the island of Manhattan, at the river's mouth. In 1626, Peter Minuit officially purchased Manhattan Island from the Native Americans. New Amsterdam – present-day New York City – founded by a Dutch merchant company, became an important center for the fur trade. The Hudson River provided easy access to the city for the Native Americans of the northeastern forests where the furs were gathered.

New Amsterdam flourished under Dutch control until 1664 when it was conquered by the English and renamed New York.

Counter-clockwise from the left:
The port of Amsterdam. In 1579 the seven northern provinces, which became the Netherlands, declared their independence from Spain, which did not recognize the state until 1648. Amsterdam was a city of merchants and a lively cultural center.

A detail of Fort Orange, in Brazil. Here the Portuguese colonial empire suffered from competition with the Dutch. The Dutch captured the city of Bahia and six other settlements by 1630.

New Amsterdam as shown in a sketch dating back to the second half of the seventeenth century. The city was founded by the Dutch in 1623. New Amsterdam became an important center for the fur trade.

THE ENGLISH IN THE NEW WORLD

Elizabethan England

The reign of Mary I, between 1553–1558, had a negative effect on England. Mary was a Catholic, and in 1534 she married King Philip II of Spain. She attempted to restore the power of the Roman Catholic church in England by persecuting English Protestants. This policy earned her the nickname "Bloody Mary." Her pro-Spanish politics led England to accept passively King Philip II's economic and political monopoly of the Atlantic Ocean. Her religious persecutions and her pro-Spanish attitude also led public opinion to identify Roman Catholicism with foreign interests.

Mary died in 1558. The new queen, Elizabeth I, who reigned between 1558 and 1603, was the daughter of Henry VIII and Anne Boleyn. She prudently achieved a change in the English approach to foreign policy and religion without resorting to fanaticism. An example of her diplomacy was the way in which she managed to modify her position regarding Philip II, who had proposed marriage to her precisely when she was beginning to counteract the pro-Spanish, pro-Roman Catholic policy of England. She not only refused Philip's offer, she also continued to refuse all other illustrious suitors, and, eventually, decided never to marry. In the field of religion, Elizabeth reestablished the authority of the Crown over the church and restored the use of the Book of Common Prayer. In this way, she reestablished Protestantism and the Anglican church.

On the international level, Elizabeth eventually clearly arrayed herself on the side of the Protestant, anti-Spanish forces. England became the ally of the United Provinces in their struggle against Spain. The English rupture with Spain was inevitable. In 1588 Philip II prepared a fleet of one hundred thirty ships, the Invincible Armada, which engaged the English fleet in the English Channel. The Spanish were driven back by English ships and destroyed by a storm.

At the same time, England began to realize the political and military advantages of being an island. It was to Elizabeth's credit that she demonstrated the best policy for her country. England stayed out of continental politics as much as possible and only occasionally helped the weaker contestant in European power struggles, just to ensure the balance of power on the continent. The experience of the war with Spain served to strengthen the political and spiritual unity of England. It mobilized England's energy toward mercantile and seafaring activities and led to a period of colonial expansion.

The English in the Americas

The privateering exploits of great explorers like Francis Drake, John Hawkins, and Martin Frobisher helped England penetrate the American continent. The efforts of Walter Raleigh led to the start of English settlements in North America in 1585, in the region the English named Virginia, in honor of Queen Elizabeth I. Raleigh's enterprise on Roanoke Island was a failure, but England had a group of leaders ready to continue the process of colonization. They were the younger sons of English landowners. They were educated and accustomed to the sea from their early childhood. In addition, there were large numbers of unemployed in England willing to emigrate. Powerful merchants, those willing to finance overseas ventures, joined forces with the representatives of the landowners. The Crown guaranteed the legal standing of the future colonies but did not wish to extend its own control directly over the new lands. The settlements would be expected to govern themselves with little interference from England.

The English settlement of North America proved extremely difficult in the beginning due to the harsh living conditions. In 1607 a group of colonists landed in Virginia on a semi-submerged island surrounded by swamps about 30 miles (48 km) up the James River. This unlikely place, named Jamestown, was the first permanent English colony in North America. The population of the colony was soon reduced by the harsh environment, Indian attacks, sickness, and general discouragement. Those who survived were bent on making a profit from the land and increasing their possessions. They desired to clear more forests, but there were not enough laborers to do the work. They devised a system of free passage from England to America for any farm workers willing to agree to work for four years without pay on the plantations. At the end of this contract period, the majority of these workers joined the ranks of tobacco growers and stayed in the colonies.

An English pirate ship attacking a Spanish galleon. The riches carried from the Spanish colonies lured pirates and privateers to attack the Spanish merchant ships.

The first English settlements in Maryland and Virginia

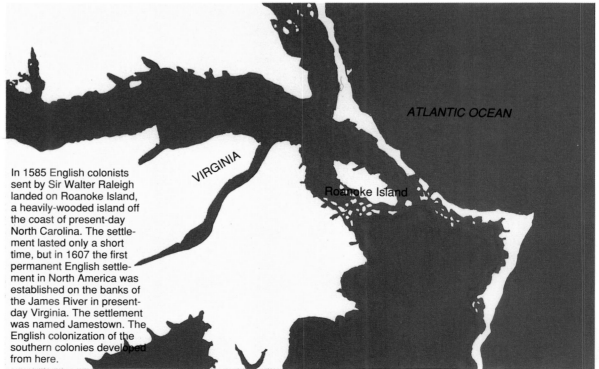

In 1585 English colonists sent by Sir Walter Raleigh landed on Roanoke Island, a heavily-wooded island off the coast of present-day North Carolina. The settlement lasted only a short time, but in 1607 the first permanent English settlement in North America was established on the banks of the James River in present-day Virginia. The settlement was named Jamestown. The English colonization of the southern colonies developed from here.

THE PILGRIMS AND THE PURITANS

The *Mayflower* and the Colony at Plymouth

Both the Pilgrims and the Puritans as religious groups drew their origins from attempts to reform the English Church. Both groups sought a more direct approach to God. Despite the break with Rome and the creation of the Anglican Church in the sixteenth century, the Puritans were convinced that the Anglican Church was still too "Catholic" and immoral. The Pilgrims developed as a separate sect in England between 1570 and 1580. They did not accept the Anglican Church and established their own churches. As a result, they were persecuted by both the official church and by the government.

In 1609 a group of Pilgrims decided to move to more tolerant Holland, where they were able to practice their beliefs freely. Gradually, however, they began to worry that their children might be too influenced by the Dutch society, which they judged as being too permissive. In 1619 the Pilgrims obtained permission from the Virginia Company to settle in its territory. They also received a guarantee from the English government that they would not be persecuted.

The Pilgrims sold their lands and property to finance their enterprise, and on September 16, 1620, they set sail from the English port of Plymouth on board the *Mayflower*. On November 21, the *Mayflower* dropped anchor in what is now Provincetown Harbor, Massachusetts. The passengers were so exhausted by the voyage they did not find the strength to continue their journey to reach the lands in Virginia which they had been promised. However, they did sail farther along the coast. On December 26, they anchored in a harbor where they decided to establish a settlement. They called their colony Plymouth.

Other settlers followed in the wake of the *Mayflower,* and by 1657 there were over a thousand colonists in Plymouth. The political struc-

ture of the colony was extremely simple. The men met once a year to elect a governor and various assistants. The governor of the colony was not, however, explicitly authorized by the Crown and was not able to create a sufficient number of new towns and churches to receive the new arrivals.

The Puritans: Power at the Service of God

The Puritans were proud, enterprising, and uncompromising with both themselves and others. The decision to emigrate to America matured between 1628 and 1630, when Puritan relationships with the English government and the Church of England had completely deterio-rated. In 1628 a group of Puritans formed the New England Company, which obtained a concession to a large part of the region known today as the states of Massachusetts and New Hampshire. In 1629 the Puritans were granted a charter by the English government to found the Massachusetts Bay Company.

In the summer of 1629, the situation in England, aggravated by an economic crisis, made the Puritans' position even more difficult. Charles I dissolved Parliament, thus making the possibility of political reform extremely remote. All Puritans with administrative positions in the government were dismissed. A group of these, made up of merchants, landowners, lawyers, and government officials, who were no longer accepted by their peers, decided to flee to North America to live according to their Puritan principles. They hoped to create a society worthy of God's approval.

March 1630 marked the beginning of Puritan emigration. During the period of greatest exodus, 1630–1643, more than twenty thousand English Puritans reached North America. The original colony, Salem, on Cape Ann in what is now Massachusetts, became the clearing station for the new arrivals. They then settled chiefly around Charlestown and Boston. Later, some Puritans established independent settlements in Hartford, Wethersfield, and Windsor, which joined together to form the colony of Connecticut.

The Pilgrims' first winter in North America after emigrating from England in August 1620 was very difficult. Many of the original settlers died. The Pilgrims, like the Puritans who followed, had permission from the English Crown to emigrate overseas where they hoped to practice their religion freely.

Indian women cultivating corn. The English learned from the Indians how to grow corn and other plants unknown to Europeans.

Products such as corn, tobacco, and potatoes, were introduced into the Old World from America. The importation of these products changed both the European diet and customs. Potatoes and corn, for example, became the staple diet of many peoples for centuries. The habit of sniffing snuff spread rapidly throughout Europe, and tobacco was imported in ever-increasing quantities.

THE FAILURE OF THE DUTCH IN NORTH AMERICA

New Amsterdam

The population of New Amsterdam grew slowly and by 1664 had reached fifteen hundred. By the middle of the seventeenth century, the village included a blockhouse, a windmill, and several houses. These were circled by a stockade, which served as a town wall, exactly where Wall Street in New York City is today. A canal ran around the edge of the settlement and about fifty small farms were scattered just outside the village.

The Dutch West Indies Company was convinced that it could continue to make a profit from the fur trade alone. The furs were easily transported down the Hudson, Delaware, and Connecticut rivers. The company officials believed it would be useless and costly to attempt the creation of an agricultural community. They were sure of earning more money, and faster, just from the fur trade. Thus, they made no serious effort to increase the population of the colony.

The War Against the Native Americans

However, back in the Netherlands, one of the company directors tried to assure a more secure future for the North American settlement. Kiliaen van Rensselaer, a rich Amsterdam jeweler, was convinced that large, private, agricultural estates should be created there. These would guarantee food, livestock, and supplies for the Dutch ships bound for the other Dutch possessions in the Americas. The result was the formation of twelve groups of financiers ready to back the creation of large farms. Only one venture was successful, the estate situated at Rensselaerswyck, on the banks of the Hudson River near Fort Orange (present-day Albany). The financier sent goods, livestock, and farm equipment to the estate. In addition, he arranged for whole families of farm workers to emigrate, at his own expense. The estate developed and survived until the end of the century.

Unfortunately, as a whole, the colony of New Netherland, which consisted of parts of what are now Connecticut, New Jersey, New York, and Delaware, was in difficulty and the governors sent by the Dutch West Indies Company were often inefficient and corrupt. One of them,

A meeting of the Sovereign Company of the Indies.

Compagnie Souveraine des Indes

named Willem Kieft, personally began a ruthless war against the local Native Americans.

The conflict began in 1642, after the Native Americans attacked several isolated farms. In retaliation, more than a hundred peaceful Native Americans camping near New Amsterdam were massacred. The war raged for three years until, in the end, the Dutch carried out a night attack on an Indian village, brutally killing and burning alive around five hundred inhabitants. A peace treaty was finally drawn up between the Dutch and the Native Americans in 1646.

The Dutch and the English

The province of New Netherland remained a region that was badly organized, badly administered, and disorderly. The lack of order was partly due to the uncontrolled multiplication of villages, which were too small to organize or defend themselves. These villages sprang up everywhere: in the upper region of Manhattan Island (New Harlem); along the banks of the Harlem River, in the area known today as Westchester County, New York; along the Hudson River, in the present-day region of Bergen County, New Jersey; and on Long Island.

The confusion was accentuated in these settlements because of conflicts with English neighbors who had moved to New Netherland from the neighboring colonies. These immigrants were attracted by the promises of freedom of worship, self-government, and free land. But the English began to rebel against the Dutch domination and demanded the English takeover of the frontier areas. The ensuing conflicts over the frontier territories became serious enough to force the colonies of New Netherland and New England to reach an official agreement in which the frontier with Connecticut was fixed at 10 miles (16 km) east of the Hudson River.

But the English colonists who had settled on Long Island continued to ignore Dutch authority, while the English in the southern part of New Netherland openly opposed Dutch rule The years that preceded the English conquest of New Netherland were characterized by continuous revolts of the English against the Dutch along the whole length of the border region.

Finally, in 1654, the Dutch West Indies Company declared bankruptcy. All that remained of New Amsterdam were several moorings, a few bridges, a ruined fort, and an abandoned town hall. The English colonists in Connecticut planned the occupation of New Netherland and invaded the frontier territories. In 1664 the Dutch colony had no resources left with which to meet the challenge of the English ships that appeared in the harbor. The English had little difficulty in conquering New Amsterdam.

A fight in New Amsterdam; an everyday occurrence in the North American settlement. After its foundation, New Amsterdam did not develop quickly, and the people made a living mainly from the fur trade. The inhabitants were people of mixed nationality and from all walks of life, who lived, worked, and often quarreled with one another.

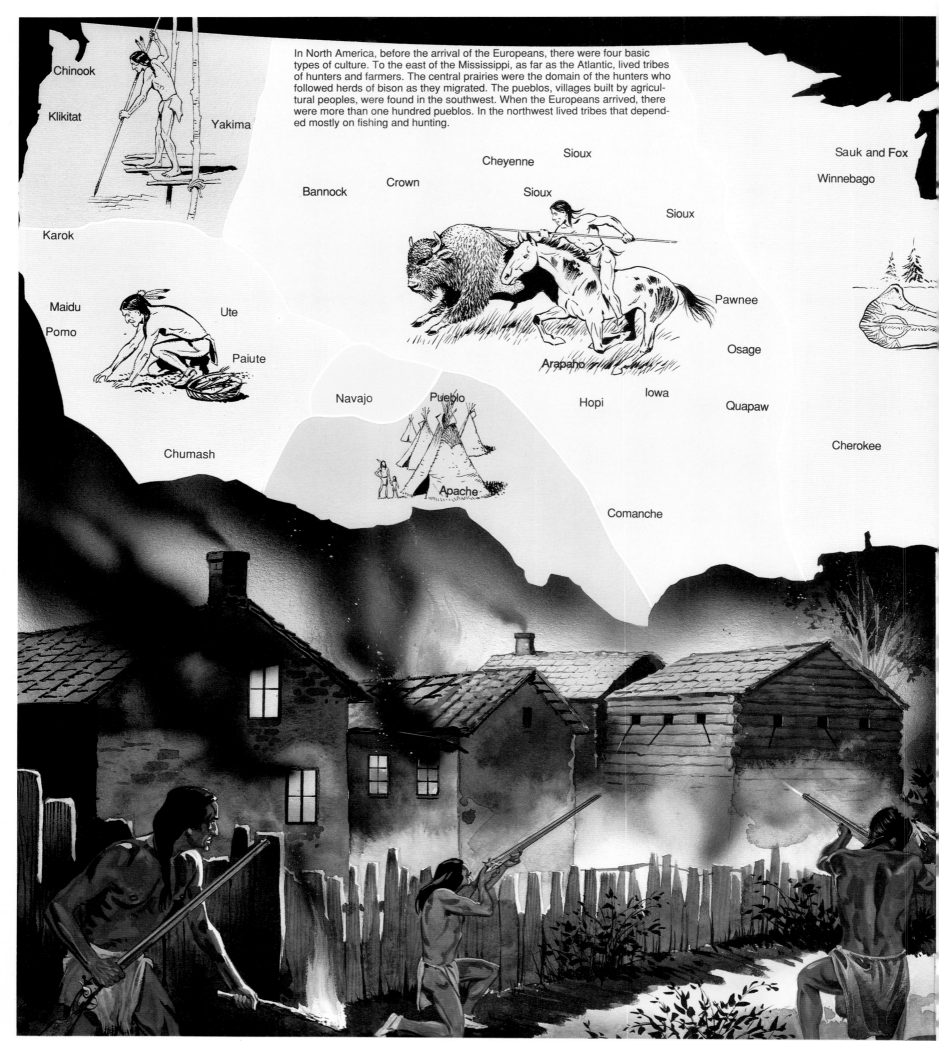

Chinook

Klikitat

Yakima

Karok

Maidu

Pomo

Ute

Paiute

Chumash

Navajo

Pueblo

Apache

Bannock

Crown

Cheyenne

Sioux

Sioux

Sioux

Sioux

Arapaho

Pawnee

Osage

Hopi

Iowa

Quapaw

Comanche

Sauk and Fox

Winnebago

Cherokee

In North America, before the arrival of the Europeans, there were four basic types of culture. To the east of the Mississippi, as far as the Atlantic, lived tribes of hunters and farmers. The central prairies were the domain of the hunters who followed herds of bison as they migrated. The pueblos, villages built by agricultural peoples, were found in the southwest. When the Europeans arrived, there were more than one hundred pueblos. In the northwest lived tribes that depended mostly on fishing and hunting.

THE ENGLISH COLONISTS AND THE NATIVE AMERICANS

Many cave drawings have been found in North America. Below are a few examples of the symbols found and their possible meanings.

Passamaquoddy
Iroquois
Ottawa
Wampanoag
Potawatomi
Iroquois
Pequot
Susquehanna
Delaware
Powhatan
Cherokee
Catawba
Creek
Choctaw
Seminole

◇	peace
●—●	conversation, communication
▲	arrowhead
⌓	far from anywhere
⌢	rain
⌒	night
⊞	the four compass points
卐	snake/demon
∿	circuit/turn
	piled
	to lift something
⌢	hill
⊙	a covered place
□	wooden object
	upward

grandfather
war
shadows
empty
heart
part
light
object
strength

Conflict Between the Colonists and the Native Americans

The colonists and the Native Americans had difficulty in understanding each other's way of life. For example, the Europeans felt Native Americans were too affectionate with their children and never punished them for their disobedience. The Native Americans, on the other hand, were horrified to see the colonists hitting their children with whips or belts. They were convinced the colonists behaved in this way to teach their offspring that the world belonged to the most violent. Even their attitudes toward work were totally different. The fur merchants, who worked for the large European companies, lived in the midst of the tribes, spoke their languages, and did everything in their power to induce the Native Americans to dedicate themselves more seriously to hunting the animals whose pelts were in demand. But the Native Americans saw little need to kill more animals than they needed to kill.

It was no easy task to convince the Native Americans to hunt more to increase the production of furs. Their total lack of greed and their lack of interest in manufactured products protected them from most forms of enticement. In the end, the merchants found that introducing Native Americans to whiskey was the most effective stimulus. As time went by, contact with the Europeans created the Native Americans' need to procure other manufactured goods, and many left their camps to live near forts or alongside the trails where the merchants' wagons passed. The Native Americans received their first guns from English and French merchants. Possessing these arms gave the eastern tribes – the first of the North American Native Americans to have had contact with Europeans – an advantage, in their periodic wars with rival tribes from the interior of the continent.

Native American Clashes with the English Colonists

In 1607 when the Virginia Company, led by John Smith, founded Jamestown, the English colonists immediately clashed with Powhatan, a powerful Native American chief in the region. After only a few years, there were no Native Americans left in the Jamestown area. The English thus clearly demonstrated their intention to take the Native Americans' lands using every means possible. Unlike the Spanish, the English had no need of Native American labor, but they did take into serious consideration the possibility of the tribes becoming potential allies in eventual wars against other European powers for the control of the American territories.

The first contacts between the Pilgrims and the Native Americans were not dramatic. When the Pilgrims settled in Plymouth, they found the area "a splendid place, suitable for the cultivation of every type of crop." However, they would have died of hunger without the help of Massasoit, chief of the Wampanoag. His authority also prevented the outbreak of war as the colony rapidly expanded toward the interior.

The first problems the Pilgrims had arose with the Pequot, a powerful tribe that lived in the Massachusetts area. The Pilgrims attacked one of their villages and massacred all the inhabitants. All the English colonies along the Atlantic coast, between present-day New York City and Boston, were dragged into the war against the Pequot. Several rival tribes also took part in the war.

Another more important war broke out in 1675 between the colonies and the Wampanoag chief, Metacom, who had also taken an English name. Since he was a chief, he was known as King Philip. The war was caused by English attempts to subjugate the Wampanoag Native Americans. Metacom was the first Native American chief to attempt to unite the tribes against the colonists. He failed, but his example was not forgotten. Later, others tried, with varying degrees of success. Overall, this war – King Philip's War – between the English and the Native Americans was the bloodiest in the history of the New England colonies. Metacom and his followers destroyed sixteen towns in Massachusetts and four in Rhode Island, and his warriors killed about six hundred colonists. In the end, though, the English prevailed. Metacom was killed, and his wife and son were sold into slavery.

Metacom's idea to unite the tribes was not completely original. As far back as the late 1500s the League of the Iroquois had been formed. Its power was never surpassed by any other Native American organization. At the end of the seventeenth century, this league dominated the region stretching from the Ottawa River in the north to the Cumberland River to the south, and between Maine in the east and Lake Michigan in the west. The league was so strong that both the English and French begged for its support during the Seven Years' War, called the French and Indian War in America.

Opposite page: One of Metacom's greatest victories was the attack and destruction of the village of Sudbury, Massachusetts. The inhabitants were all killed. Captain Samuel Wadsworth pursued the Native Americans but was killed in an ambush.

Center: The Portuguese voyages of exploration in Africa marked the beginning of the slave trade. The white merchants usually bought slaves from the rulers of the coastal states. As shown in the picture, the slaves were captured in organized raids into the interior villages.

Top of page: A brass plate showing the figure of a Portuguese warrior (Benin, sixteenth century). Until the mid-sixteenth century, the slave trade remained in the hands of the Portuguese. They had commercial bases scattered along the coastal strip of western Africa.

Below: A golden Ashanti mask dating back to the fifteenth century (*London, Hartford House*). This African kingdom had originated in the eleventh century. The slave ships set sail from its coast.

THE SLAVE TRADE

African Slaves

The Portuguese voyages of exploration and discovery in Africa also marked the beginning of the slave trade with the western hemisphere. Until the mid-sixteenth century, this traffic remained in the hands of the Portuguese who had bases scattered all along the west coast of Africa. The contractors who supplied the slave ships operated from there. As a general rule, the white slave merchants did not procure the slaves directly but bought them from the rulers of the states along the coast. These sovereigns organized raids on the villages in the interior or even sold their own subjects to the Europeans in return for firearms.

These unfortunates were forced aboard ships to face a terrible voyage. They traveled in special ship holds, at most $3\frac{1}{4}$ feet (1 m) in height. The slaves were chained together and had very little space in which to move around. The ships were designed to be able to carry the largest possible cargo. The slaves were crammed in this way, not only to ensure the highest possible profit per voyage, but also to give them the least physical opportunity to revolt. The mortality rate for voyages undertaken in these conditions was between 20 and 30 percent. The slaves died from privation, illness, and severe beating. There were also many cases of both individual and mass suicides.

The Spanish government did not want to be directly involved in the slave trade. However, the Spanish granted contracts for the importation of slaves, charging a tax for every slave who entered their American dominions. The slave trade from Africa to America grew as the cultivation of sugarcane increased. African slaves also replaced South American Indian laborers, whose numbers had been drastically reduced due to the hard work in the mines and the ravages of diseases.

With the increase in demand – a direct consequence of the extermination of the Native Americans – the slave trade flourished. A commercial triangle was established. European manufactured goods were sent to Africa where they were exchanged for slaves, who were then sold in the Americas. The final stage was the acquisition

A plan showing how slaves were loaded on a slave ship. The purpose was to cram in the greatest number of people.

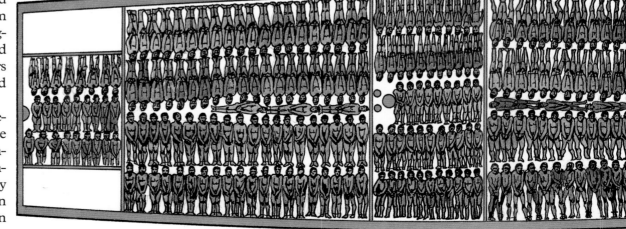

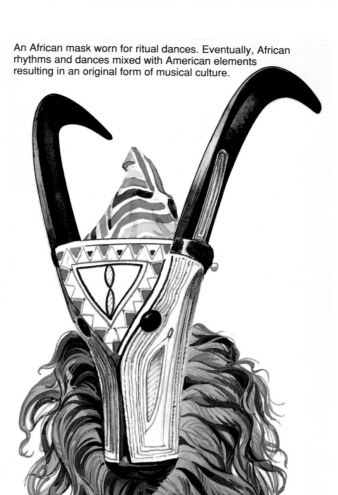

An African mask worn for ritual dances. Eventually, African rhythms and dances mixed with American elements resulting in an original form of musical culture.

of American raw materials from the colonies for importation to Europe. Gradually, the Portuguese slave ships were joined by Dutch, French, Danish, and Swedish vessels.

The Employment of Slaves in Latin America

The way the slaves were distributed throughout the different regions in America depended on the type of economy in each. African labor was used on the sugar, cotton, and tobacco plantations. The slaves also worked in the mines. Many others worked as domestic servants and in various branches of the crafts. Their physical resistance to disease often depended on the climate of the place where they were sent. For example, in mines situated in the high mountains, many slaves from the internal tropical regions of Africa fell victim to disease. Africans found the climate similar to that of the sultry, humid Caribbean islands and the coastal plains of South America more hospitable. In the West Indies, slaves replaced the indigenous population which had been killed off. In the mountainous regions, their ability to survive was greatly reduced, and in the Andes, for example, the African element of the population almost completely disappeared.

It is difficult to calculate exactly how many Africans arrived in America. The most reliable estimates speak of around fifteen million. The importation of slaves was a typical feature of all the colonization of the New World. Some voices were raised in protest against slavery, but even Bartolomé de Las Casas was, at first, in favor of slavery as a way of alleviating the plight of the Native Americans.

Slaves in North America

Slavery began in North America in the early 1600s, and the traffic in slaves increased very rapidly after 1700. Originally, slaves were brought in from the West Indies, but by the 1670s slaves were being imported directly from Africa.

Living conditions for slaves on many plantations in the English colonies were extremely degrading. Often the slaves did not live in huts or cabins, but in barrackslike dwellings, where it was impossible to live a normal family life. In time, the increase of the black population led to the development of more stable communities. Some of the following generations managed to avoid working in the fields because of the need for craft workers and servants. This produced a form of culture that was a mixture of traditional African and European-colonial elements. Once it had formed roots and begun to flourish, it became part of the national culture of the American people.

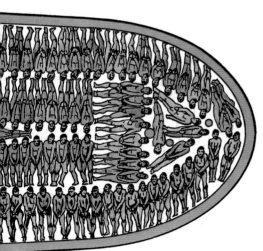

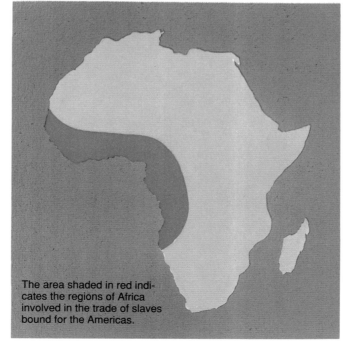

The area shaded in red indicates the regions of Africa involved in the trade of slaves bound for the Americas.

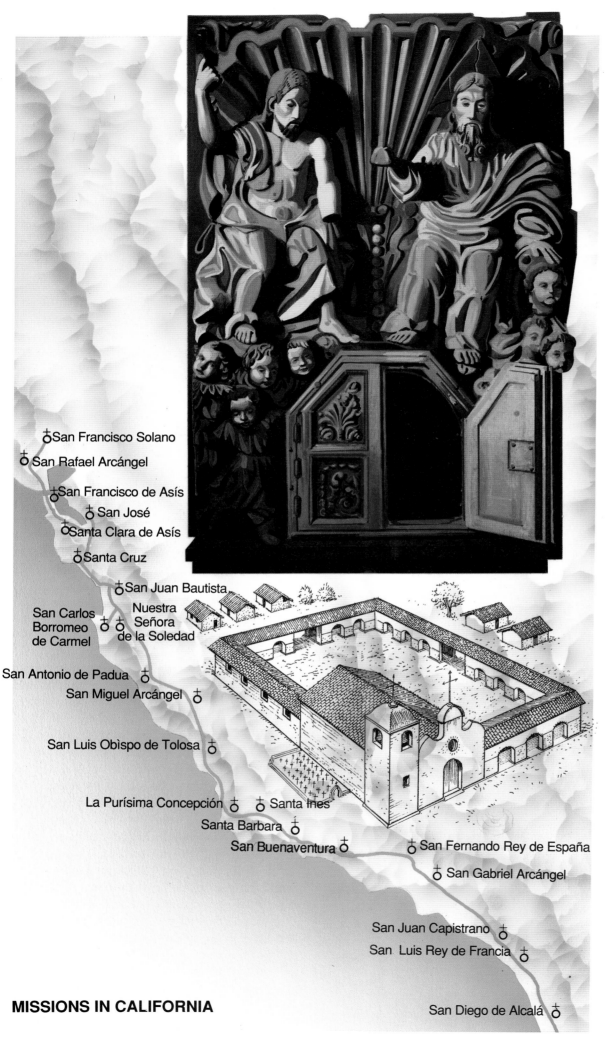

Center page: The Spanish captain, Juan Pardo, meeting an American Indian chief in Florida. The start of the Spanish occupation of Florida dates back to the second half of the sixteenth century.

Map: The map shows the location of the Franciscan missions along the coast of California. The missionary orders played a fundamental role in the exploration of the central and northern regions, often preceding the arrival of the Spanish army. In some regions the missions were the only European presence. The sketch shows the basic design of a mission.

Left: A wooden tabernacle from a California convent church. The Native American population helped to build and decorate the mission churches and buildings. Local craft workers combined their traditional techniques and decorations with elements from the Christian religion.

San Francisco Solano

San Rafael Arcángel

San Francisco de Asís

San José

Santa Clara de Asís

Santa Cruz

San Juan Bautista

San Carlos Borromeo de Carmel

Nuestra Señora de la Soledad

San Antonio de Padua

San Miguel Arcángel

San Luis Obìspo de Tolosa

La Purísima Concepción

Santa Ines

Santa Barbara

San Buenaventura

San Fernando Rey de España

San Gabriel Arcángel

San Juan Capistrano

San Luis Rey de Francia

San Diego de Alcalá

MISSIONS IN CALIFORNIA

THE SPANISH IN NORTH AMERICA

The rise of strong nations in northern Europe marked the beginning of the Spanish decline on that continent. However, the Spanish managed to expand and defend their American dominions due to a series of circumstances. In the seventeenth century, the northern European powers had only a marginal interest in the Americas. Their struggles within their own countries prevented them from paying more attention to the Americas and from taking advantage of the vulnerable Spanish position there. Furthermore, Spain's enemies were involved in wars with each other.

Florida was explored by the Spanish during the second half of the sixteenth century. Several conquistadors and missionaries explored the interior of this region without establishing any kind of permanent settlement. The region was, however, of strategic importance, because Spanish fleets, bound for Spain, sailed near Florida's western coasts. Moreover, when the French in 1564 moved into the area and founded Fort Caroline at the mouth of the St. Johns River, Spanish occupation of the region became imperative. The following year, the Spanish established a fort which they named St. Augustine. Today St. Augustine is the oldest permanent European settlement in North America.

Missionaries played an important role in the consolidation of the Spanish dominions. The Franciscans created two lines of missions in Florida. The missionaries ranged as far north as South Carolina and west to the southern end of the Appalachian Mountains.

Northern Mexico

The search for new silver mines was the direct cause of Spanish expansion into northern Mexico. These mines were situated in the semiarid prairies along the eastern flank of the Sierra Madre. The region was populated by nomadic Native Americans. As had already occurred in Florida, the Franciscans spearheaded the Spanish advance, winning the friendship of the natives. During the sixteenth century, this area was opened to colonization, and mineral fields were developed at Durango, Charcas, San Luis Potosí, and Parral. Farms were developed in the more accessible valleys where water was plentiful. These farms produced corn and grain crops to feed the miners. Cattle ranches began to prosper in the more arid areas. Frequently, the mine owners also owned the farms and ranches. Their descendants managed to keep and increase their lands, transforming them into huge estates called *haciendas*. The hacienda housed the owner's family, together with priests, overseers, craft workers, *vaqueros* (cowboys), and domestic servants. Spanish expansion in northern Mexico was strongly stimulated by the ambition to create vast estates.

Toward the middle of the seventeenth century, the Spanish Crown granted substantial financial help for the colonization of the state of Nuevo Leon in northern Mexico. Missions and military garrisons were built also in eastern Texas, which the Spanish were later forced to abandon due to Native American resistance.

Baja (Lower) California

The missionary orders played a fundamental role in the Spanish expansion into both northwestern Mexico and Baja California. The Franciscans, followed by the Spanish colonists, reached the upper Rio Grande. The Jesuits followed the Sonora River as far north as Arizona.

The Jesuits also established missions in Baja California, where the coastal waters had already been renowned for pearls at the time of Cortés. The Crown encouraged colonization, but the Spanish were discouraged by the arid terrain.

New Mexico was also colonized by the Spanish, but Indian revolts regularly drove away the colonists and the missionaries. The repression of the Native American revolts in New Mexico was a long and difficult task.

The principal ethnic groups of emigrants to the English regions of North America.

English

Dutch

French

German

Irish

Scotch

African

This porcelain object made in New England in the seventeenth century is the work of a German emigrant. In the colonies of North America, each ethnic group continued to dress and live according to the customs of their native land.

ANGLO-AMERICAN SOCIETY IN THE EIGHTEENTH CENTURY

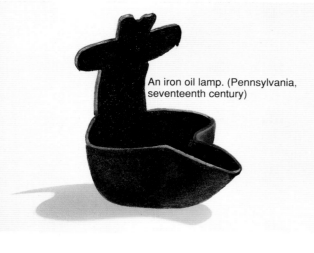

An iron oil lamp. (Pennsylvania, seventeenth century)

By the beginning of the eighteenth century, the colonists from England had established themselves on the North American continent. The English colonies formed an almost continuous line along the Atlantic coast from New Hampshire to Georgia. Toward the interior, the colonists had reached the point of the first set of rapids on each river that flowed out to the ocean. The population at this time totaled around 250,000 people. The inhabitants were of European or African birth, or descent, and for the most part, English-speaking. However, the population of the colonies was not distributed uniformly. It was concentrated along the Atlantic coast and in the river valleys. Thus, many areas remained uninhabited and uncultivated by Europeans. Even in Massachusetts and Virginia, the colonists, for the most part, continued to live like frontier pioneers. Many colonists had actually been born on American soil. The colony was their homeland, even though they knew their grandfathers had come from a more powerful European nation much farther away. If they did not yet think of themselves as Americans, they had a way of life that was increasingly different from the European model.

The Population

Most of the free population of the English colonies was composed of poor workers from England. They were neither vagrants nor social outcasts. They were more often farmhands, unskilled workers, and crafts workers. Except in New England, many of the white immigrants had arrived as indentured servants. They had agreed to work for four or more years for a person in return for their ocean passage to the colonies. When they were free of these obligations, they often bought or were entitled to receive land of their own.

Free people in the colonies were much more mobile than they had been in Europe. There were few legal limits to control their movements, and everyone was free to go almost anywhere they wished. The population increased rapidly, while in Europe at this time, national populations grew little, if at all.

The Economy in New England

At first, the New Englanders did not wish to become involved in transoceanic trade. The Puritans had no desire to keep links with a world they had left behind. They hoped the new communities would soon become economically self-

sufficient. However, the attempts to create a self-sufficient economy failed. Around 1650 the Puritans created a complicated economic system, linked to transoceanic trade, which remained until the American Revolution. The production of flour, fish, and lumber for construction developed rapidly in New England. The commercial prospects this offered soon became clear. These products would not be sold to England, where they were already produced, but to France and the Spanish American colonies. All the fish sent from New England was sold in these places, and in the West Indies other foodstuffs needed to feed the work force were also sold. Both lumber for building and horses used for power in the process of producing sugar were sold throughout the American continent. They were exchanged for sugar-based products which found an easy market both in the colonies and back in England.

Other regions became involved in this circle of trade: Virginia produced tobacco; New England became an important source of fish; New York and Pennsylvania produced a variety of agricultural products. Thus, a commercial system developed in New England which, with certain variations, was adopted by all the northern colonies.

Several circumstances made this trade vigorous but difficult to forecast. First, the local production of the goods to be sold was irregular. Bad harvests were frequent. Furthermore, it was difficult to know exactly how much could be sold in the West Indies.

In this colonial world there was no precise definition of commercial class. Anyone could set up a business as there were no legal barriers to prevent their doing so. The government encouraged the growth of trade.

The Economy of Southern Colonies

The early economy of the southern colonies was based on tobacco. Low prices and unforeseeable variations in both the production of tobacco and the market for it conditioned the product's development. The tobacco trade was in the hands of merchants from London who penalized the planters if crops failed. Tobacco production depended on a large work force, and slavery seemed the obvious solution to this need for field hands.

In the Anglo-American world it was often difficult to preserve social differences. On the farms in both northern and southern colonies, the lifestyles of the owners, laborers, ministers, and professionals were very similar.

A New England farm. Life on the farms was very hard at the beginning. The owners and the laborers lived in very similar ways. There was no time in which to be idle.

ART IN LATIN AMERICA

St. Francis' church in Acatepec. The Mexican baroque style is typified by the eye-catching decoration of surfaces, a combination of Spanish and Native American artistic experiences.

The Baroque

The term baroque indicates an artistic style popular in Europe, and subsequently, in America during the seventeenth century. The origin of the term is not clear. It would appear to derive from the Portuguese word *barroco* – a type of irregularly shaped pearl, having many facets. During the second half of the eighteenth century, the word became synonymous with irregular, bizarre, or unequal shapes. Consequently, when applied to the fields of painting, sculpture, and architecture, the term baroque indicated a style that paid little attention to proportion.

The Baroque style, with its richness, plus the artists' preference for spectacular scenic effects, spread rapidly in Europe. The most successful aspect of the style was the new idea regarding space. There was a real feeling of dimension and texture. Surfaces were covered with elaborate designs and carvings. In Spain and Portugal, the baroque style combined with the rather flatsided building style current at the time. This resulted in buildings with extravagantly decorated facades.

Latin American Colonial Art

When discussing colonial art in Latin America, we must keep in mind that the immigrants to the New World brought with them the cultural heritage of Romanesque, Gothic, and Renaissance art. During the first century of colonization, the mixture of these styles led the way toward the birth of Latin American baroque. Regional American styles developed throughout the seventeenth century as new styles of art from Europe continued combined with elements of Native American, Creole, and mestizo art.

The colonial art of Latin America was not, therefore, the mere transfer of European styles to the New World. The natural artistic gifts of the Native Americans, their sense of form and color, and the colonists' fascination with a land so aesthetically different from Europe tended to modify the artistic styles imported from the Old World.

The European version of baroque architecture is complex. It depends on the principles of optical illusion. Buildings in Spanish America have a relatively simple structure but are more elaborately decorated.

The originality of the Latin American baroque style is often to be found in its ornamental details. For example, the habit of decorating shields with feathers was maintained. The Native Americans' skill in working with precious metals led to the creation of extravagant jewelry. The interiors of buildings together with decorative objects were often enriched with magnificent inlay work. In fact, the Latin American baroque style found its most original expression in the decoration of wood.

The Latin American baroque style was used above all in religious art. Religion and colonization were closely linked in Latin America. The missionary orders reached into many regions, and the Franciscans, Dominicans, Augustinians, and Jesuits played an important part in the history of colonization.

Mexican Baroque

A large part of what is termed Mexican baroque can be recognized by the eye-catching decoration of surfaces, the result of the Native Americans' artistic experiences accumulated during the centuries before Columbus arrived in America. The local influences combined with the Spanish flat-sided building style. A typical example of this fusion of styles is the cathedral completed in 1661 in Mexico City.

The Mexican baroque style is the first example of an original colonial Mexican style of art. Previously, Mexican art had almost completely limited itself to repeating the art forms imported from Europe.

A model of a typical Central American city built in the Latin American baroque style. The construction of the cities began very early in the colonization period. The Spanish government made general rules for the foundation of settlements. For example, the plan of the city was to be like a chessboard. These rules were not always observed. In contrast with the elaborate decoration of the churches, the civic architecture was fairly simple.

A section of the decoration of the narthex of the Church of St. Francis in Quito, Ecuador. The design resembles Indian themes, such as the sun, together with Arab themes, such as decorations, and is evidence of the influence of Spanish culture.

BAROQUE ART IN SPANISH AND PORTUGUESE AMERICA

The Sculptors of Quito

In the colonial era, the province of Quito occupied the territory of present-day Ecuador. Less than fifty years before the Spanish conquest, the city of Quito was the second capital of the Inca Empire. The other was Cuzco. The Franciscans were the first to settle in the province. In 1530 the Convent of St. Francis was founded. A college destined to educate the sons of the more important local Native Americans was annexed to the convent. The curriculum included instruction in and practice of several art forms, and of sculpture in particular.

The most famous artist in Quito was the mestizo sculptor Bernardo Legarda, who had a workshop beside the Franciscan monastery. Legarda created the statue that decorates the high altar in the monastery church. Moreover, he created many artistic works dedicated to the Virgin Mary in a period when visions of saints were a part of religious life, and artists prepared themselves for their work with prayer and fasting. Incidents from the life of the Virgin Mary were very popular subjects among artists of the time. The artists of Quito were particularly fond of the themes surrounding the story of the Virgin's Assumption to Heaven. They were especially clever at creating ecstatic facial expressions and at carving praying hands in a very delicate way.

Legarda produced his work in the first half of the eighteenth century. The most important sculptor from Quito during the second half of the century was Caspicara. His real name was Manuel Chili, and his parents were Native Americans. Even though many aspects of his work are similar to the work of Legarda, it is difficult to prove if he was actually a student of the earlier sculptor. However, the continuity of style between the two artists demonstrates the depth and high level of the sculpting skills taught during the first thirty years of the eighteenth century in Quito.

Caspicara lived during the late baroque period, when porcelain and ivory ornaments were highly appreciated decorations in colonial houses. Many of his works are busts or groups of sculptured figures. For this reason, he is considered more of an innovator than Legarda, who mostly produced single sculptured figures.

Caspicara's most important work is the Assumption, which decorates the altar dedicated to St. Anthony in the Church of St. Francis, in Quito. In this work Caspicara showed he was capable of giving a unifying theme to a group of sculptured figures, while producing richly detailed single figures at the same time. Caspicara's work in general gives the spectator the impression of movement.

Baroque Art in Brazil

For a long time Brazil remained a colony of little importance, valued only for its high quality lumber. The Portuguese Crown found this land disappointing compared with the rest of Latin America, and there was very little active settlement. This explains why Brazilian architecture was much plainer than the architecture of colonial Spanish America up until the baroque era. The baroque period coincided with the discovery of precious metals in Brazil. The products of the mines – silver and gold – were used to decorate churches and other buildings.

The city of Ouro Prêto (Black Gold) has many excellent examples of the use of gold and silver in works of art. The city was named after the gold found in the black rocks of the surrounding hills. Its thirteen churches, numerous public buildings, decorated fountains, and pleasant avenues, linking the hills to the city, make it an open-air museum. Many houses are adorned with figures and have window frames resembling those found in eighteenth century churches. When they were built, the balconies had railings and wooden shutters that formed geometric patterns. Glazed tiles were imported from Portugal and the Netherlands. They were used because of the shiny quality they gave to roofs. One of the city prisons is so well decorated that the iron bars at the windows are hardly noticed.

The splendor of these buildings is witness to the mastery of the local crafts workers. Their skill is especially evident in the Church of the Rosary, in Ouro Prêto. The roundish, oval forms of the plan and the facade are a brilliant example of the use of curved lines so typical of baroque architecture.

The crafts workers from Quito produced works like this richly decorated pulpit in the Church of St. Francis, Quito, Ecuador.

Top left: A column from the facade of a Jesuit church in Quito. Top right: An ornamental altar column from the Church of St. Francis in Quito.

A sixteenth century cross, set with emeralds (*Central Bank Museum, Ecuador*).

Quito, Ecuador.
The cloister of the Church of St. Francis.

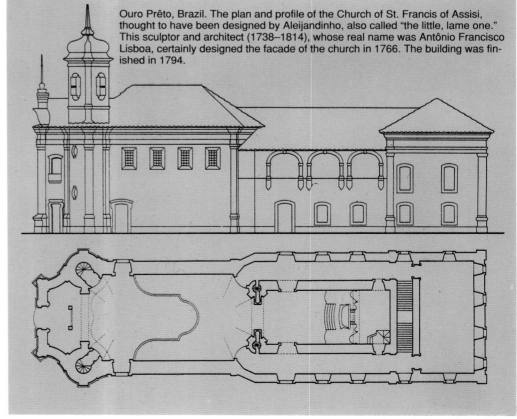

Ouro Prêto, Brazil. The plan and profile of the Church of St. Francis of Assisi, thought to have been designed by Aleijandinho, also called "the little, lame one." This sculptor and architect (1738–1814), whose real name was Antônio Francisco Lisboa, certainly designed the facade of the church in 1766. The building was finished in 1794.

SPANISH AMERICAN ECONOMY

Agriculture and Livestock Breeding

Despite the discovery of gold and silver, the agricultural land continued to be the chief natural resource of Latin America. A large part of the region was more suitable for raising livestock than for farming.

The Europeans claimed small, medium, or large-sized lots of land. The Spanish Americans acquired properties called haciendas, which ranged in size from small farms to vast estates. The most important haciendas were situated in northern Mexico, in the valleys of central Chile, and on the slopes of the Andes.

In the more densely populated areas and near the larger towns, the smallest haciendas grew cereals crops and reared a few animals, both destined to be sold in the local markets. In the tropical and subtropical regions, the haciendas tended to specialize in cultivating sugar, cacao, and indigo.

Already at the beginning of the seventeenth century, Spanish America had become self-sufficient in the production of wheat and other cereals. The creation of more pastureland also guaranteed a large reserve of meat. Vines and olives flourished in the river valleys of Peru and central Chile. These regions produced wines and olive oil of a fair quality, much cheaper than what was produced in the Old World. They sold so well in Spanish markets that the Spanish king was pressured by the wine and olive oil producers in Andalusia, Spain, into curbing any further expansion of the cultivation of these products in the Spanish American territories and prohibited their exportation to Spain.

Besides the principal foodstuffs, the most important farm products were hides, sugar, cacao, tobacco, and cotton. Spanish America was also able to draw on several products from the forests: lumber and bark containing colorants, flavors, like vanilla beans, many types of spices, and medicinal plants. Taken together, all these products formed a large part of the total colonial exports to Europe.

Capital and Industry

The Spanish Americans certainly appreciated the value of money, but the quest for riches was considered only part of a more complex way of life. The wealthy spent a large proportion of their resources on donations to the church, dowries for their daughters, and a luxurious life-style. It was not their custom to trust their money to banks or to buy shares in businesses.

In spite of this attitude, small businesses developed to meet the needs of the colonial marketplace. Food processing, pottery, and the manufacture of articles from hides grew in proportion to the growth of this internal market. The textile industry underwent the greatest development. There were basically three main reasons for this: the expansion of the internal Spanish American market, the weakness of the

textile industry in Spain, and the high cost of textile products imported from Europe.

At the beginning of the seventeenth century, hundreds of workshops throughout the West Indies manufactured clothes and other textile articles. Ecuador was the main center of production in South America, due to its large herds of sheep and large labor force. The looms produced woolen cloth, cotton, silk, linen, and hemp. The majority of the workshops were privately owned, but in Mexico and Ecuador some were owned by Native American communities.

The Spanish colonies were self-sufficient in the production of low and medium quality textiles, but a variety of circumstances prevented the American textile industry from expanding more fully. The Spanish government issued a series of laws regulating textile production and conditions for the employment of labor. The labor laws were intended to protect the Native Americans from exploitation. However, the government's desire to reduce competition from the colonial industry in favor of the domestic market was the real reason behind the legislation. The Spanish Americans invented many ways to avoid the restrictions, but Spain's action certainly slowed down the expansion of the colonial industry.

Taxation

Interference from Spain had a negative influence on the development of the economy in Spanish America. Beginning in the reign of Philip II, the government adopted fiscal measures regarding the economy of the Spanish American territories. Driven by the rising costs of wars, Spain introduced a series of taxes. There was a general sales tax, a tax on stamped paper, on mercury, salt, pepper, and on all forms of trade.

Smuggling

Spanish producers were not able to satisfy all the needs of the American market. Furthermore, the goods exported from Spain were too expensive. On the other hand, Spain was unable to absorb colonial products at a price that was acceptable to both producers and consumers. This set of circumstances forced the Spanish American traders to start smuggling as a solution. Meanwhile, the Dutch and English undertook the organization of an international trading community developed in the Caribbean area. English, Dutch, French, and Spanish merchants traded with each other, heedless of government restrictions. It was also during this period that direct trade, bypassing Spain, began to develop between the Spanish American colonies and the northern European nations.

Left: Work in a Cuban sugar refinery. The growth and processing of sugarcane continued to be one of the chief resources of the West Indian economy.

Right: A cattle ranch. The expansion of ranching caused an increase in the production of foodstuffs. Already at the beginning of the seventeenth century, the Spanish territories in America could count on a plentiful supply of meat.

SPANISH AMERICAN SOCIETY

Throughout the colonial era, the Spanish living in the Americas believed their society should be divided into classes. They felt, moreover, that this type of class structure should be sanctioned by law. The social classes they intended to establish, such as nobles, clergy, ordinary citizens, were traditionally European. However, by the end of the period of conquest, the American reality was already different from what the Europeans had imagined. The Spanish government opposed the creation of a powerful class of nobles in Spanish America. Furthermore, there was no category in the traditional class system that might include non-Europeans, that is to say, the majority of the American population.

For these reasons, while the social order in the Spanish American territories of the New World did in fact have a class structure, the distinctions were based on race. The Spanish considered themselves physically different from Native Americans, from Africans, and from those of mixed backgrounds. This physical difference, combined with the cultural differences, justified, in their eyes, severe forms of discrimination between the groups.

Independent of their class or origin, the Spanish considered themselves the direct descendants of the conquistadors and defined themselves as *gente de razón* – rational beings who belonged to an ordered society. They believed their superiority was also evident from their physical characteristics. They saw themselves as robust, vigorous, and fair-skinned. Legally, they enjoyed several privileges. The encomenderos, who were more or less the heirs of the conquerors and the first colonists, formed the most aristocratic group in Spanish colonial society. Meanwhile, a new aristocracy had emerged, made up of the owners of the haciendas. Owning land was no automatic guarantee of prestige and honor, but it was the necessary condition to begin climbing the social ladder. The great landowners had a stable work force, lived for part of the year in luxurious city dwellings, and managed to obtain positions in local government.

The old and new aristocratic groups occasionally came together through marriage. In this way the encomenderos acquired haciendas, while the haciendas became related to families more established than their own. But from the moment the encomiendas began to disappear, and the haciendas became larger and more numerous, owning land became the most common way to be accepted as part of the nobility.

Ordinary Citizens

The merchants held the highest position in the social scale among the Spanish who did not belong to landed or noble families. The rich importers and silver merchants of Mexico City and Lima formed associations that dealt directly with the representatives of the Spanish king in America. The mercantile associations were also popular among the common people because they financed the construction of hospitals, orphanages, and roads.

Other groups belonging to the class of ordinary citizens increased as the years went by. Lawyers and notaries belonged to this class and were engaged to document, discuss, and judge an ever–increasing quantity of law suits. The next level of the hierarchy was composed of crafts workers, shopkeepers, small farmers, and domestic servants. The lowest class was made up of poor laborers and vagrants.

The Clergy and the Royal Bureaucracy

From the seventeenth century on the power of the Roman Catholic church increased enormously. The foundation of new cities and the development of those already in existence required the creation of new parishes. The church also owned a great deal of land and enjoyed the respect and devotion of all the faithful.

The king's official representatives in Spanish America formed an important part of the Spanish American population. They enjoyed a high level of social prestige and were often ennobled on their return to Spain.

A Spanish American wedding. Marriage was often a means of uniting the old aristocracy of the *encomenderos* with the new aristocracy, formed by the *hacendados*.

A beautifully decorated, lacquered plate (Seventeenth century, Ecuador).

CHARACTERISTICS OF THE SPANISH AMERICAN WORLD

The Native Americans

On the whole, the Spanish considered Native Americans not only uncivilized and ignorant, but also lazy, unreliable, and incapable of really becoming Christian. The Spanish classified the natives according to their physical characteristics. They were smaller and not as sturdy as the Europeans. Their hair was straight, and their skin was darker than that of the Spanish.

The Indians had to pay taxes to their masters, and their freedom of movement was limited by law. However, in response to the rapid decline of the native population, the Spanish government expressed concern for the welfare of the remaining Native Americans and gave them special status as wards of the monarchy. The Spanish king continued to appoint high ranking civil and church officials as protectors of the Indians. These people were granted special rights. The most important provision was the creation of special courts for the Indians. These courts dealt especially with trials involving disputes between Indians and Spanish or proceedings between Indians.

The Indian population had its own particular social structure. The highest class was composed of the descendants of members of the noble classes in pre-Columbian times. The Spanish government recognized these nobles, granting them certain privileges and immunity from several restrictions. However, this class gradually lost its importance, the aristocrats became poorer, and it was increasingly difficult to distinguish between them and other groups in the Native American population.

There were two other classes among the Indians who were not of noble descent. The largest was made up of those Native Americans obliged by law to live in fixed communities and to pay taxes. The second group consisted of those Indians who fled their villages and settled at the edges of the larger cities or on the haciendas as farm laborers.

Mestizos, Free Blacks, and Slaves

By the end of the seventeenth century, two centuries of mingling between the races had produced a population of mixed background in the Americas. This was chiefly made up of mestizos, children of Europeans and Indians; mulattoes, children of European and African parents; and zambos, children of Indian and African parents. This portion of the American population was considered as a single class by the Spanish. The Spanish regarded them as idle, vagrant, loose, and insolent. They were seen by the Spanish as a threat to religion and public order. The more their numbers grew, the more the fear of the Europeans increased. Yet, some tried to better themselves by obtaining honest jobs, living in one place, and contracting lawful marriages.

These different groups were treated by the Spanish government in a similar way to the Native American Indians. They were obliged to pay taxes, and their freedom of movement was very limited. They also were not allowed to carry weapons or go to a university.

Although slavery of the Indians continued in secret, from the seventeenth to eighteenth centuries, the majority of the slaves were blacks and mulattoes. Even though they were all considered the same by the law, differences gradually began to appear among the slaves themselves. Those who lived as servants in the houses of the rich Spanish, together with artisans, were considered a kind of aristocracy. Those who worked in the mines were considered socially lower in class both by the Spanish and by the remainder of the slave population.

How Changes Were Made

Social and class differences were well fixed in both Spanish law and Spanish mentality, but they were not unchangeable. Slaves could achieve freedom in various ways. They could buy their freedom by paying a certain sum or be declared free if their master was proved guilty under the law of mistreating them.

Social class was determined not only by the color of a person's skin, but also by their way of life. In this way some mestizo families often managed to mix with members of the Spanish lower classes. The practical needs of the state also contributed to social leveling. In order to boost the army, for example, the rules forbidding the recruitment of persons of mixed background or of blacks were waived. As a general rule, the whiter the skin, the easier it was to change one's social class. However, access to the higher social classes in the Spanish American world remained largely impossible for non-whites.

Even after the Native Americans' conversion to Roman Catholicism, ancient rituals survived throughout Latin America.

Left-hand page: A witch doctor celebrating a ceremony and receiving a nutritious drink in return from the faithful. The Indians of the Western Sierra Madre were converted to Roman Catholicism, but worshiped in their own way. For example, some still believe even today that Joseph won the right to marry the Virgin Mary by playing the violin in a competition.

Right-hand page: The Flying Dancers, a ritual still in use today by the Totonac tribe in Mexico. The man on top of the pole is the captain of a team and represents the sun. At his signal, four men seated at his feet launch themselves backward into the air. They are held by strong ropes. They represent the four basic elements: earth, air, water, and fire. Since the conversion of the tribe to Roman Catholicism, this ritual is celebrated on the anniversary of the birth of St. Francis of Assisi. The ritual is presented as it was in the past, and the festival is a mixture of Christian elements mixed with traditional rites.

The garden of a colonial villa in New Spain. The master is giving orders to two black slaves. A nurse, carrying the master's son in her arms, chats with a mestizo domestic servant.

The presence of non-European peoples helped loosen the ties between the Creoles and Spain. Indians, blacks, and mestizos introduced some of their traditions into the Creole way of life.

THE CREOLES

The Spanish and the Creoles

A wide rift divided the European-born Spaniards from those born in America. The Spaniards born in Europe called the American-born Spanish Creoles. This title soon acquired a negative sense. The European Spanish thought that being born in the Americas automatically created defects in a person's character. They found the Creoles irresponsible and unpredictable. The Creoles themselves were offended by the arrogant, patronizing attitude, typical of most of the new Spanish arrivals in the colonies. Moreover, they resented the ease with which these Spaniards often managed to acquire important positions and other advantages, which by law should have been given to them. Despite this, the American-born Spanish tacitly accepted the social superiority of those who came from Europe.

The Creoles

The first Spanish who arrived in America had no doubts regarding their identity, but those who remained, slowly grew less certain. The conquerors dreamed of returning to Spain covered with glory, fame, and riches, and of becoming important landowners and part of the nobility. But the spoils of the conquest fell below their expectations, and so many stayed in America. As time passed, their attachment

being born in the Americas and celebrated their way of life. They described their land as lush and generous and praised the beauty of their cities, the splendor of their buildings and churches, and the success of their commerce. They considered themselves energetic, highly imaginative, hospitable, and courteous. The Creole writers affirmed that the American culture had no reason to envy the culture in Spain. Behind these declarations was hidden the desire to contradict the insults they received from the Spanish-Europeans. The Creoles aimed at creating a Creole spirit, a pride in being a Spanish American, and a freedom from an inferiority complex regarding Spain.

The Creole identity was especially evident in the context of religion. The Creoles thought themselves the most devout of all Catholics. A great deal of their time was spent at mass or celebrating baptisms and Communion services. They frequently made donations to their parishes or local convents and regularly made generous offers to charitable institutions. During the seventeenth century, a series of apparently miraculous recoveries from illness and reports of religious visions led the Creoles to believe that God had decided to reward them for their particular dedication to religion. In 1671 the first American saint was canonized. The Creoles were granted a small number of bishoprics and provided the Catholic church in America with several higher church officials.

Regional Differences

The different types of Spanish American peoples were the result of a mixture of geographical and demographic factors. The Native American culture was more protected in the high plateaus, where the large population could preserve the old ways. Creole society developed well in the same regions because their groups had deep roots there and controlled the economy. On the plains and in the areas near the ports, the Creoles tended to keep stronger ties with Europe, due to their dependence on transoceanic trade.

The most elaborate and complex social groups were found in the high river basins and valleys of the great mountain ranges. These regions were inhabited by a large number of Indians and mestizos. The regions, however, were dominated by a white minority of powerful aristocratic families who made the rest of society bend to their will.

The Spanish American colonial world was more simply organized in the regions of the plains, where the population chiefly consisted of an ever increasing mixture of ethnic backgrounds. These regions were also the poorest areas, where the social differences due to wealth were less evident.

to the land they had conquered became stronger. Their children, the true Creoles, felt a deep sentimental attachment to the land of their birth. Its sights, sounds, and smells were dear and familiar to them. Their physical well-being depended on the mines, the farms, and the products from the New World.

The presence of non-European peoples contributed to loosening the ties with the Old World. The Creoles' houses were filled with sounds foreign to Spanish ears. Their Castilian Spanish was mixed with gentler sounding words and accents. As babies they were cared for by

Native American wet nurses, and as children they ate food with exotic local ingredients. Native herbalists calmed Creole fevers with ointments and herbal teas, and native crafts workers decorated Creole churches with pictures of the animals and plants of the Americas. However, the Creoles felt a certain nostalgia for Spain, mixed with a sense of inferiority because they could not consider it their real native land. But they also felt a certain rancor toward the new arrivals from Europe.

The Creoles began to develop their own culture. Creole authors expressed their pride in

BRAZIL

Brazil and Portugal

The colonial government in Brazil was military in structure, dominated by the governors and their subordinates. During the eighteenth century, when exploitation of the rich Brazilian gold mines began, the Portuguese government attempted to control the political and economic life of the colony more closely. Overall, though, the government in Brazil was smaller in scale and less complex than in Spanish America.

Brazilian Colonial Society: The Ruling Classes

The coastal regions where sugarcane was cultivated, from Pernambuco to Rio de Janeiro, were the most highly developed areas of the colony. The Portuguese made up the dominant class. Within these regions, the owners of the plantations formed the leading class and were also appointed to the government positions. The officials sent by the government in Portugal enjoyed privileges and titles that set them above the other social groups, but they did not have the power to dominate the local aristocracy.

Immediately below this class in the Portuguese American society came a kind of middle class, made up of the merchants involved in foreign trade. They lived in the most important ports and were usually of European birth. They were not the richest members of society, and they were dominated by the plantation owners. However, the most wealthy among them purchased land or married into one of the landholding families and became part of the landed aristocracy. The plantation owner-merchant, who divided his time between his activities on the plantation and the demands of the market, became an important part of the social structure.

The most modest European social class in colonial Brazil was made up of shopkeepers, crafts workers, accountants, small farmers, and the superintendents and technicians who worked on the plantations. As in Spanish America, Brazilian society was deeply divided according to people's place of birth – the Portuguese born in America, or Creoles, and those born in Europe.

The Creoles were deeply attached to Brazil. They were proud of the beauty of the country and with the generosity of its land. The Portuguese language they spoke began to include words of Native American and African origin. Their African cooks used the products of the New World to invent a typically Brazilian cuisine.

African colors, sounds, and rhythms were present in the religious celebrations of the colony and continue to this day.

The Lower Classes

Both the Creoles and the Portuguese born in Europe considered the Africans and Native Americans inferior beings because of their so-called primitive origins. These prejudices led to the condemnation of marriages, between Europeans and Africans or Native Americans and to the restriction of movement and freedom of choice regarding work.

The children of Native Americans and Portuguese suffered a little less from racial discrimination. They were free and considered to be nearer to the Europeans due to the color of their skin. The free blacks and the mulattoes were placed on a lower level in the social scale. For this reason, they were not allowed to occupy positions in the church or in the civil government. The lowest class was formed by black and mulatto slaves.

People of African origin were more numerous in Brazil than in Spanish America, and they lived in larger groups. The slaves often escaped and fled to the uninhabited interior of Brazil where they formed communities. During the seventeenth and eighteenth centuries, ten large groups of this type existed in the interior. The strongest group called their territory the Republic of Palmares. The inhabitants built stockades and erected dwellings inside their walls. They created an artificial lake, well-supplied with fish. The refuge that Palmares offered to slaves from the plantations represented such a threat to the owners of the great plantations in Pernambuco that the army was forced to intervene. The settlement resisted at length and fell only after a siege lasting forty days in 1697.

The Society of the Hinterland

A different type of society developed in the northern Brazilian hinterland and on the southern plateaus. These vast regions of desert, brushwood, and prairie were populated by Europeans, Africans, and Native Americans, who gave life to a population of mixed heritage.

Another type of society developed in the Amazon region. The Portuguese reached this area at the beginning of the seventeenth century and during the following years consolidated their claims to the Amazon River basin. A few scattered settlements appeared after the initial explorations. The inhabitants were merchants both of Portuguese or mixed background, harvesters of products from the forest, missionaries, natives under missionary care, and Indians who had remained independent.

Left-hand page:Large Brazilian plantations were called *fazendas.* The great *fazenda* owners made up the dominant class in Brazil. They were also given government positions.

Below: A street in São Luis do Maranhão, Brazil. Royal officials lived in the city and also landowners who preferred to take personal charge of the sale of their products.

MISSIONARIES IN THE AMERICAS

The *doctrina* and the *congregación* were the two institutions especially created by the missionaries to help them in their conversion of the Native Americans to Roman Catholicism in Spanish America. The *doctrina* was a school for religious instruction housed in a convent. Here young people were taught the catechism. Some young people were accepted as boarders in the convents and received a more intensive type of training. They were in turn expected to help teach their own people.

The *congregaciones* were Native American communities organized by the missionaries. Apart from facilitating their religious conversion, these communities aimed at transforming the Native Americans' way of life. The missionaries intended that the Indians adopt European habits. They were supposed to learn to eat at the table with the proper instruments, to sleep in beds, and to give up drunkenness.

The missionaries also attempted to ease the Indians' physical suffering. To this end, hospitals were built using native labor. The poor and travelers passing through the area were also welcomed in these institutions.

The missionaries encountered numerous difficulties. The regions entrusted to the monks were too vast to be controlled easily. The Indians often refused to abandon their traditional dwellings, and those who were forced to enter the Christian communities often fled. The missionaries regularly disagreed with important landowners in the area because the missionaries saved the natives in their care from exploitation.

The Jesuits in America: The *Reducciónes*

The Society of Jesus was founded in Spain in 1539. It differed from the other missionary orders in its lack of racial and social prejudice. In fact, its members came from all levels of society. Rather than fleeing the world, the Jesuits aimed at becoming more involved in it.

In their missions, the Franciscans taught the Indians farming skills, how to tan hides, and how to improve their traditional crafts.

They were especially involved in the education of the young.

The Jesuits arrived in the Americas later than the other missionary orders. They built on the experience of the congregaciones. They persuaded the Indians to live in groups of villages called *reducciónes*. The name derived from the Latin expression, *reducere ad ecclesiam et vitam civilem,* which means "to lead towards the church and a civil life." A church was built in the center of the community, and the priests taught their assistants the basic ideas of the faith. To make their task easier, the Jesuits learned the natives' language. The Indians usually lived in the reducciónes but accepted the idea of true conversion with difficulty. They often continued to worship their old gods and kept many of their old customs.

At first the reducciónes were founded near the cities. In Brazil, for example, the first communities were created near Bahia, Pernambuco, and Rio de Janiero. These reducciónes were often attacked by the Indians who had not been converted and by Portuguese colonists, who wanted to use the Indians of the reducciónes as slaves. Both the Jesuits and the Portuguese government opposed the idea of exploitation of Indians. New reducciónes were constructed in regions far away from the European settlements. They were self-sufficient and out of bounds to whites, except for the Jesuits.

This type of community could be found in a vast area including parts of the present-day countries of Paraguay, Uruguay, Argentina, and Brazil. Some of the reducciónes were often attacked by armed gangs who destroyed the communities and took the Native Americans prisoner. In Paraguay, the Jesuits obtained the Spanish Crown's permission to arm the Indians under their protection. In 1641 an army of four thousand Guaraní Indians inflicted a crushing defeat on the plunderers. The Jesuit province of Paraguay then began to enjoy a period of calm and prosperity, and by the end of the eighteenth century, there were thirty flourishing reducciónes in the region.

Below: Bandits raiding a reducción to capture the Indians who worked there. The reducciónes were founded by the Jesuits to keep the Indians from being exploited as slaves.

The plan of a reducción. The community was made up of a church, Indian dwellings, storehouses, and cultivated fields. The most important Jesuit reducciónes were situated in Colombia, along the upper Orinoco River, in Peru, along the upper reaches of the Amazon and the Marañón, and along the Paraná River, in Paraguay.

The Market Place in New Orleans.

NEW FRONTIERS IN NORTH AMERICA

In the second half of the seventeenth century, England made a greater effort to control the life and organization of its American colonies, but failed to create one central office responsible for coordinating all the government offices with interests in the colonies. The English government remained an accumulation of different government bureaus, often in conflict with each other, and, consequently, the nation's control over its colonies remained weak. Economically speaking, the empire was run on mercantile principles. These were translated into law via the Navigation Acts, which attempted to regulate commerce.

In 1760, when George III became king, the colonists celebrated the event with enthusiasm. The colonists, as subjects of Great Britain, enjoyed the most liberal political conditions in the western world. They foresaw a free and prosperous future. However, during the long years of settlement, development, and the search for stability, several areas of conflict had accumulated between Great Britain and its colonies. The most obvious areas of conflict were caused by the various wars that had been waged by England against other European nations.

The War of Jenkins' Ear and King George's War

In the eighteenth century, Britain fought three wars against the other European powers, and each war also involved the colonies.

The War of Jenkins' Ear (1739-1742) was fought against the Spanish over trading rights in the colonies in the Caribbean Sea and Central America. With the peace treaty in 1713, which marked the end of the War of Spanish Succession, Britain had obtained the right to sell a certain number of products in the Spanish West Indies. The presence of British vessels also brought an increase in smuggling, which the Spanish tried to restrain by stricter cargo inspections. An Englishman, Captain Robert Jenkins, was caught smuggling and had his ear cut off as punishment. War broke out after this episode. A colonial American regiment, led by English officers, was recruited for an expedition against Cartagena, Colombia. Most of the money to finance the expedition was also collected in the American colonies. Due to the incompetence of the officials, the

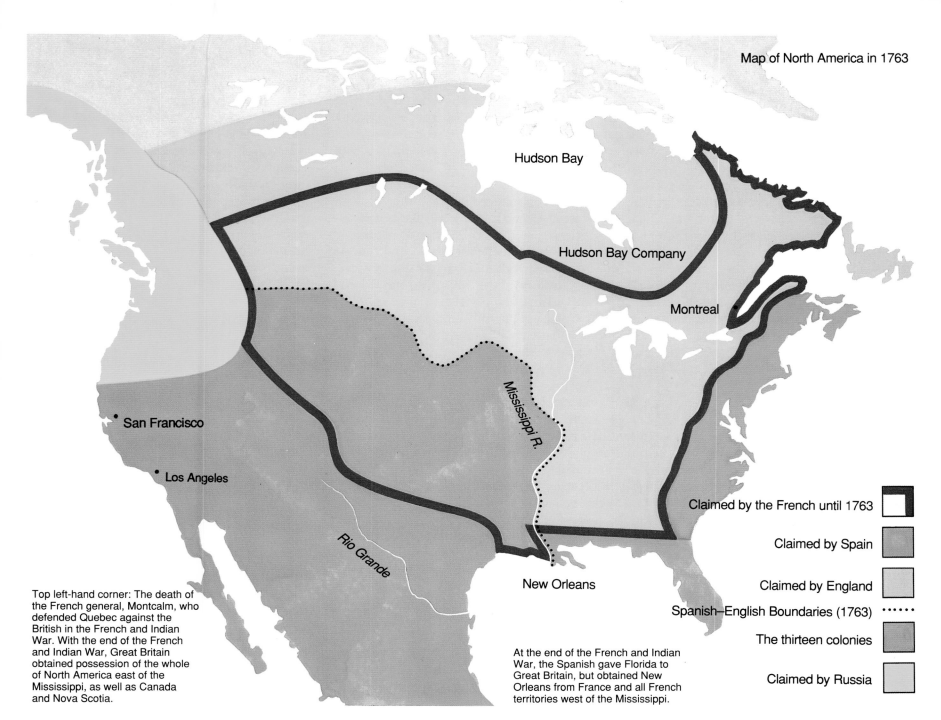

Hudson Bay

Hudson Bay Company

Montreal

San Francisco

Los Angeles

Mississippi R.

Rio Grande

New Orleans

Top left-hand corner: The death of the French general, Montcalm, who defended Quebec against the British in the French and Indian War. With the end of the French and Indian War, Great Britain obtained possession of the whole of North America east of the Mississippi, as well as Canada and Nova Scotia.

At the end of the French and Indian War, the Spanish gave Florida to Great Britain, but obtained New Orleans from France and all French territories west of the Mississippi.

Claimed by the French until 1763

Claimed by Spain

Claimed by England

Spanish–English Boundaries (1763) ••••••

The thirteen colonies

Claimed by Russia

campaign was a disaster. Only six hundred American soldiers survived.

In 1740 another war against the Spanish broke out in Europe. Through a complicated series of conflicts and alliances, Great Britain tried to prevent continental Europe from falling under the control of one single power – France. The conflicts between 1740 and 1748 are known in Europe as the War of Austrian Succession. In America, the conflict was called King George's War (1744-1748).

In America, the war was fought around the French base of Louisbourg on Cape Breton Island. Britain had declared war against France in 1744, and the governor of the Massachusetts colony organized the attack against the fortress of Louisbourg. All the colonies sent equipment and troops, and the Americans captured the French base. It was a great victory for the colonies. But, when the peace treaty was drawn up in Europe,

in exchange for the return of Madras, India, from the French, the British gave Louisbourg back to the French. It seemed as though five hundred Americans had died for nothing to capture the naval base.

The French and Indian War between 1756-1763 was known in Europe as the Seven Years' War. In America, it broke out with a series of clashes between the French and the Virginians over the settlements in the Ohio River valley. The British suffered two years of defeat. Finally, William Pitt, Minister of War, organized an army of twenty-four thousand British and twenty-five thousand American soldiers. The plan was successful, and the French forces were defeated.

When the war ended in 1763 Great Britain held undisputed possession of the whole of North America east of the Mississippi River, excluding New Orleans, but including Canada and Nova Scotia. Spain, which had been

France's ally in the war, gave Florida to the British, but obtained New Orleans and territories to the west of the Mississippi.

Great Britain had accumulated an enormous debt to cover the expenses of the war. This debt forced George III to impose new taxes on the colonies. This was one obvious negative effect of the war. The Americans rejoiced in the victory. Their frontiers were no longer threatened by the French or Spanish. However, during the war, the colonists had realized they were a different people from the British. They had been struck by the arrogance of the British officers together with their lack of preparation. They resented above all the rigid imperial reinforcement of British Navigation Acts which were designed to raise money from the colonies. The merchants and several colonial politicians began to understand that some of the links with Great Britain might be counter to American interests.

THE BRITISH COLONIES ON THE EVE OF INDEPENDENCE

In the British colonies of North America, a century and a half of development had drastically changed the way of life inherited from Europe. During the eighteenth century, Great Britain began to interfere, suddenly and forcefully, with the life of the North American colonies. The most obvious cause of tension between Great Britain and the colonies was the resentment generated by trade laws, which were considered hostile and arbitrary by the Americans. Another important cause of tension was the Americans' feeling that, although they were in many ways different from people in Great Britain, they still had the same rights as Englishmen but were not being treated as equals. This attitude could change the course of history just as much as battles and laws could but is much more difficult to measure and describe.

The Americans

During the period of growth and expansion before George III came to the throne, the Americans gradually became aware of having a somewhat separate identity from the British. This difference was not so much embodied in their laws or politics, but rather in the character and culture of the people. The Americans considered themselves simple, innocent, rustic, unsophisticated people. The English also considered them this way, but often judged the same characteristics more as failings than as virtues.

There were practical reasons that helped spread the idea of Americans as simple and innocent people. This impression was encouraged by the propaganda used for the recruitment of potential emigrants from Europe to the colonies. For more than a century, leaflets and publications had been circulating in Europe and America with the aim of attracting emigrants. This form of advertising described

the marvels of a simple, benevolent society, where the king's power was reduced and where land could be claimed by anyone willing to farm it. The colonies were seen also as a land where freedom of religious practice was more or less allowed.

This religious tolerance was symbolized by the success in America of the Puritans and – above all – the Quakers. In the 1680s the members of this religious sect, led by William Penn, had settled the colony of Pennsylvania and founded Philadelphia, "The City of Brotherly Love." Philadelphia prospered from its foundation. It was open to everyone and became an important cultural center. Within just one generation, Philadelphia became the most dynamic city in the whole of British America, with some ten thousand inhabitants.

During the seventeenth century, the Quakers had been considered religious extremists. They were famous in England for their independent intellectual spirit and for their total refusal to respect governmental authorities. They showed little prejudice and accepted people from all social classes. The atmosphere of the eighteenth century was more tolerant, and the Quakers' reputation improved. They were no longer the fanatical defenders of religious freedom, but they did support religious tolerance and human rights when both were threatened by the arrogance of the establishment.

Both Pennsylvania and British North America as a whole became the example of a society free from the hindrance of rigid institutions. It was a simple society, but of a high cultural level, as embodied in the figure of Benjamin Franklin, the son of a soap manufacturer, but also a self-taught genius and scientist who could speak on equal terms with the major thinkers of his day. For much of the western world, Franklin represented the essence of America; a simple land but well able to teach something to the Old World.

This symbol of a divided snake was drawn to show the need for the union of the thirteen British colonies. This symbol became popular during the American Revolution.

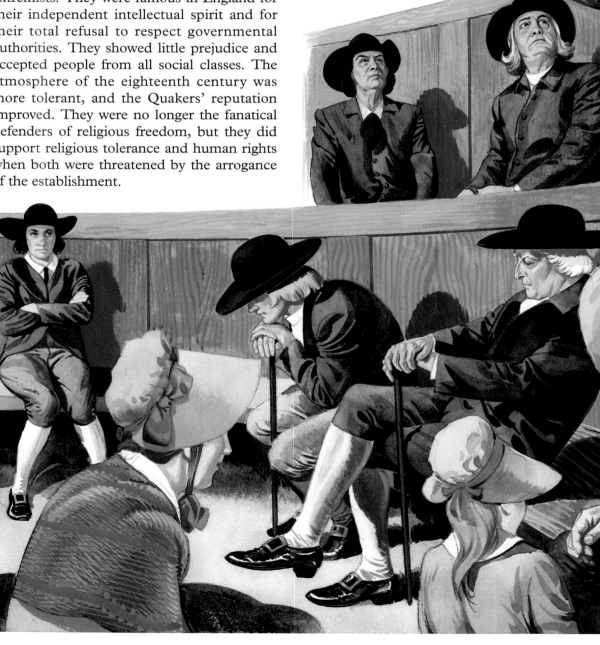

A Quaker meeting. During the eighteenth century, the Quakers were considered supporters of religious tolerance and human rights.

A New York market place toward the end of the eighteenth century. Gradually, the Americans began to see themselves as different from other peoples and as having a separate identity from the British. They considered themselves as simple people, who lived in a freer land than Great Britain. In America anyone could acquire land, live where they wished, and practice the religion of their choice, usually in more freedom than in Europe.

An Inuit. The northernmost regions of North America remained unexplored by Europeans for a long time.

A caravel.

Walter Raleigh. His efforts led to the foundation of the first English settlement in North America (1585).

A conquistador.

Quebec

Montreal

New York

Boston

Philadelphia

A Quaker.

San Francisco

Los Angeles

A typical Cuban colonial mansion.

New Orleans

Mexico City

A Mexican church, built by the Jesuits in 1600.

Thirteen colonies

Claimed by England

Claimed by Spain

Claimed by Russia

America About 1763

The two maps illustrate the political situation present on the two American continents on the eve of American Independence.

The people and objects illustrated beside the maps symbolize the effects and innovations the Europeans brought to the Americas.

Christopher Columbus

Quito

Lima

Pernambuco

Bahia

Ouro Prêto

Rio de Janeiro

Santiago

Buenos Aires

A black slave.

Spanish territories

Portuguese territories

British territories

Dutch territories

French territories

Unexplored areas

GLOSSARY

Aleut: a native of the Aleutian Islands and western portion of the Alaskan peninsula

archipelago: a sea with groups of many scattered islands

aribal vase: an Inca vase used for transporting liquids

arquebus: early kind of portable gun, supported on a tripod or a forked rest and detonated by the use of a fuse, before flintlock muskets were invented

artisan: skilled worker in industry or trade

astrolabe: navigational instrument used in the Middle Ages to determine the height of the sun

Baroque: florid or extravagant style in the arts (especially architecture) in Europe in the seventeenth and eighteenth centuries

bastion: part of a fortification that stands out from the rest; military stronghold near hostile territory

blockhouse: military stronghold with openings through which to shoot

captaincies: a large area in a Portuguese colony given to a person to establish a colony

cinerary urn: a burial urn used in ancient times to preserve the ashes of the dead after cremation

cloister: covered walk on the sides of an open court, especially in the grounds of a convent, cathedral, or college

concession: right given by owner(s) of land, or by a government to do something on or with the land, for example, to take minerals from the land

conquistador: one of the sixteenth century Spanish conquerors of Mexico and Peru

Creole: person of European descent in the West Indies or Spanish America; person of mixed European and African ancestry in the West Indies

decimate: kill or destroy a large part of a group, a population, for example

deity: state of being a god or goddess

despot: a ruler with absolute power

edict: order or proclamation issued by authority; decree

facade: (architecture) front or face of a building, toward a street or open place

facet: one of the many sides of a cut stone or jewel

Gothic: style of architecture common in Western Europe in the twelfth to sixteenth centuries, characterized by pointed arches and clusters of columns

hemp: plant from which coarse fibers are obtained for the manufacture of rope and cloth

hinterland: remote parts of a country away from the coast or a river's banks

indigo: deep blue dye obtained from a plant

Inuit: Native American group living in northern Canada, Alaska, and Greenland; the word means "the people."

manioc: tropical plant with edible, starchy roots

mendicant order: religious order of friars obtaining a living by asking for alms (money, food, clothing)

mercantile: relating to trade, commerce, and merchants

mestizo: person with one Spanish parent and one Indian parent

mulatto: person who has one white parent and one black parent

omen: sign of something good or warning of evil fortune

papal bull: official order or announcement from the pope

polygamy: custom of having more than one wife at the same time

possession: a country's overseas colony

pre-Columbian: before Columbus' journey to America

privateer: a privately-owned armed ship that, with open or unspoken government approval, attacks the ships, especially merchant ships, of another nation; also, the captain of such a ship

pulpit: raised and enclosed structure in a church, used by a clergyman, especially when preaching

Renaissance: period of revival of art and literature in Europe in the fourteenth, fifteenth, and sixteenth centuries, based on ancient Greek culture

Romanesque: style of architecture, with round arches and thick walls (in Europe between the classical and Gothic periods)

scurvy: diseased state of the blood caused, especially among sailors of former times, by eating too much salt meat and not enough fresh vegetables and fruit

sextant: instrument used for measuring the altitude of the sun, in order to determine a ship's position

snuff: powdered tobacco, taken into the nose by sniffing

INDEX

(Place names and identities in maps and in captions are included in this Index.)